Basic
Sunday School
Work

Harry M. Piland

CONVENTION PRESS

This book is the text for a course in the subject area
Sunday School Leadership of the Church Study Course.

Dewey Decimal Classification Number: 268
Subject Heading: SUNDAY SCHOOLS

Printed in the United States of America

CONTENTS

FOREWORD

This book deals with fundamentals. It describes what is essential if a Sunday School is to be the kind of vigorous, outreaching, Bible teaching organization that will help a church fulfill its God-given mission.

Because it deals with basics it should be studied by every Sunday School worker and potential worker. It is a reference book as well as a concept book. If the more than one million Sunday School workers in the churches affiliated with the Southern Baptist Convention will follow the suggestions in this book, then the Bold Mission Thrust goal to share the gospel with everyone in the world by the year 2000 can become a reality.

Sunday School work is dynamic. Much has changed since the publication of *Working in Sunday School* and the age-group "Working" books in 1974. The tasks of the Sunday School have been revised. Age-group suggestions have undergone change. Curriculum materials have been added. All of these revisions have been made to help your church meet the challenges of the 1980s.

In 1978 Harry M. Piland was elected as the leader for the Southern Baptist Sunday School program to succeed A. V. Washburn, who had given over forty years of service to his denomination, the last twenty as director of the Sunday School Department of the Sunday School Board. This book contains the dreams and hopes of Dr. Piland.

Dr. Piland came to the Sunday School Board from twenty-five years of service in four growing churches. The suggestions in this book grow out of the conviction that there is a direct relationship between Sunday School enrollment increase and number of persons won to the Lord and baptized into the fellowship of a church.

It is our hope that this book will help you build a vibrant, growing Sunday School, which helps your church do God's work in your community.

Ernest R. Adams

ACKNOWLEDGMENTS

Scripture quotations marked "Phillips" are reprinted with permission of Macmillan Publishing Co., Inc. from J. B. Phillips: *The New Testament in Modern English,* Revised Edition. © J. B. Phillips 1958, 1960, 1972.

Passages marked "RSV" are from the Revised Standard Version of the Bible, copyrighted 1946, 1952, © 1971, 1973.

Quotations indicated by "NASB" are from the *New American Standard Bible.* Copyright © The Lockman Foundation, 1960, 1962, 1963, 1971, 1972, 1973, 1975. Used by permission.

Quotations marked "NEB" are from *The New English Bible.* Copyright © The Delegates of the Oxford University Press and the Syndics of the Cambridge University Press, 1961, 1970. Reprinted by permission.

Verses marked "Williams" are from *The New Testament, a Translation in the Language of the People,* by Charles B. Williams. Copyright 1937 and 1966. Moody Press, Moody Bible Institute of Chicago. Used by permission.

Passages shown as "TLB" are taken from *The Living Bible.* Copyright © Tyndale House Publishers, Wheaton, Illinois, 1971. Used by permission.

Quotations marked "GNB" are from *The Good News Bible,* the Bible in Today's English Version. Old Testament: Copyright © American Bible Society 1976; New Testament: Copyright © American Bible Society 1966, 1971, 1976. Used by permission.

Part I

FOCUS ON MISSION

Chapter 1

The Sunday School Is . . . Seeing the Mission of the Church

"For God has allowed us to know the secret of his plan, and it is this: he purposed long ago in his sovereign will that all human history should be consummated in Christ, that everything that exists in Heaven or earth should find its perfection and fulfilment in him" (Eph. 1:9-10, Phillips).

"That you may declare the wonderful deeds of him who called you out of darkness into his marvelous light" (1 Pet. 2:9, RSV).

"That repentance and forgiveness of sins should be preached in his name to all nations" (Luke 24:47, RSV).

"You shall be my witnesses in Jerusalem and in all Judea and Samaria and to the end of the earth" (Acts 1:8, RSV).

These words of Scripture communicate clearly that the church has a mission to fulfill. That mission is a global mission given by the Lord Jesus to the church, which he established. That mission has not been cancelled nor have the orders to the church been withdrawn.

With the mission Christ gave the church came the power needed to accomplish that work. "All authority in heaven and on earth has been given to me . . . . lo, I am with you always" (Matt. 28:18,20, RSV). "Behold, I send the promise of my Father upon you" (Luke 24:49, RSV). "You shall receive power when the Holy Spirit has come upon you" (Acts 1:8, RSV). The church is commissioned by Christ and it is sustained by his power on the authority of the Father. Christ left his work in the hands of an empowered church fully capable of doing his work through his Spirit.

Let us consider, then, the nature of the church established by our Lord.

THE NATURE OF THE CHURCH

What is the church? For anyone who confesses Jesus Christ as Lord and Savior, this question is of utmost importance. For to "be in Christ" (2 Cor. 5:17; Rom. 8:1; Phil. 3:9; 1 Cor. 15:22; Eph. 1:14) is to be incorporated into his body, which is the church. To ask "What is the church?" is for the Christian as basic as a person's understanding of himself, the nature and origin of his family, his cultural background, and his national distinctives.[1]

Several concepts are embodied in the nature of the church.

Assembly.—In the New Testament, the word *ekklesia* is used to refer to the body of believers in Christ. This term derived from another word, which means "the called-out ones." When it was used by Greeks, it meant a gathering of people called out from their homes into some public place for the purpose of discussion. Certainly this word picture is appropriate to refer to the early church and today's churches. We are called out for special purposes, to do the work of God.

The people of God.—This term is used to refer to a fellowship of persons who live under the kingly rule of God. The church is the people of God, who have responded to his call to do his redemptive work in the world. The church, as the people of God, refers to the overall fellowship of the redeemed regardless of time or place (Acts 8:1,3; 12:1; 1 Cor. 15:9; Gal. 1:13; Phil. 3:6).

The church in a local sense.—Most of the references to the church in the New Testament are to specific bodies of believers in various localities. No doubt this is because individual churches were being addressed and cited in the epistles particularly. In any event, the New Testament certainly underscores the fact that local bodies of believers did and still exist to do the work of Christ in the world. Hobbs maintains that a local church is simply the visible operation of the general church in a given time and place.[2]

This church in a given place is a body or assembly acting under the lordship of Christ and directing its own work. The local church administers the ordinances and cooperates in sending our missionaries to share the gospel with the nations of the world. In Baptist life, it is the local congregation on which we focus most of our attention.

The church as a body.—The church also is fittingly and beautifully described as a body with Christ as its head. Paul made this point clear to the Ephesians: "He put all things in subjection under His feet, and gave Him as head over all things to the church, which is His body" (Eph. 1:22-23, NASB). We see the same truth in Colossians 1:18 and Romans 12:4-5. In 1 Corinthians 12:12-27, Paul described in even greater detail the figure of the church as the body of Christ. The body, though made up of many members varying in sizes and functions and differing in age and ability, still works together under the leadership of Christ.

So then, a church lives! It is not a lifeless organization. As the body of Christ, it is his agent to carry out his work.

The church as a spiritual temple.—Paul wrote to the church in Corinth, "Do you not know that you are God's temple and that God's spirit dwells in you?" (1 Cor. 3:16, RSV). "In the Old Testament we have the material Temple, the Temple built of wood and stone. In the New Testament we have the spiritual temple, built of living stones, redeemed men and women: 'Ye also, as living stones, are built up a spiritual house' (1 Pet. 2:5)."[3]

The church is a spiritual temple because Christ dwells in the church. It is this indwelling of the Spirit that makes the church the living body of Christ. The church has a mission to fulfill, and the nature of the church is compatible with that mission. Let us look closer at that mission.

THE MISSION OF THE CHURCH

Mission is inherent in the very nature of the church. The church cannot be true to its nature without being on mission. The church is the agent of the Holy Spirit to carry out the mission of our Lord Jesus Christ. The mission of the church is to confront the nations of the world with the gospel. The mission of the church more specifically is to evangelize the people of the world (Matt. 28:18-20; Luke 24:44-49). The mission of the church is to be "witnesses both in Jerusalem and in all Judea and Samaria and even to the remotest part of the earth" (Acts 1:8, NASB). The mission is clear, direct, and positive. And we respond to that gigantic mission with commitment and faith.

We conclude then that the mission and purpose of the church is to carry out the will of Christ in the world. We can identify specific functions of the church in carrying out the will of Christ. Those functions may be summarized as worship, proclamation and witness, nurture and education, and ministry.

Worship is the foundation stone. Encounter with God empowers God's people for encounter with others. All other functions of the church are vitally related to worship. When we worship, we become truly aware of God's presence within us. When we worship, we adore, confess, and pray to the Father through his Son. John quoted Jesus: "An HOUR is coming, and now is, when the true worshipers shall worship the Father in spirit and truth; for such people the Father seeks to be His worshipers" (John 4:23, NASB).

All members of the body are responsible for proclamation and witness. The church places high priority on this function, as indeed it should. The Word of God is proclaimed when the church is gathered and on other occasions when the church is represented by the preached word. Witness, on the other hand, may be thought of as one individual sharing his witness or testimony with another. Each of us has a testimony and witness to share. Witnessing takes place as the scattered church shares its faith with individuals.

Nurture and education are clearly found in the latter part of our Lord's commission as he instructed: "Teaching them to observe all that I commanded you" (Matt. 28:20, NASB). The Bible is to be taught. Its meaning is to be made clear. The Word of God is to be taught in a way that causes persons to encounter God, respond to him in faith, and learn to live by that faith. The disciples are to grow and develop in God's grace and in a Christian life-style. Indeed, the "discipled" are to become the "disciplers."

Ministry also is included in the latter half of the Great Commission. Jesus said his disciples were to observe all the things he taught (commanded), and the church has received the pattern of ministry from the life of our Lord. For indeed he "went about doing good" (Acts 10:38). He loved, cared, healed, and had compassion on the multitudes; and he instructed his disciples to follow his example. The Savior revealed his heart to us when he said "to the extent that you did it to one of these brothers of Mine, even the least of them, you did it to Me" (Matt. 25:40, NASB).

Ministry was and is a part of the mission of the church.

THE IMPORTANCE OF THE BIBLE IN THE MISSION OF THE CHURCH

The Baptist Faith and Message statement expresses clearly what Baptists believe about the Bible:

"The Holy Bible was written by men divinely inspired and is the record of God's revelation of Himself to man. It is a perfect treasure of divine instruction. It has God for its author, salvation for its end, and truth, without any mixture of error, for its matter. It reveals the principles by which God judges us; and therefore is, and will remain to the end of the world, the true center of Christian union, and the supreme standard by which all human conduct, creeds, and religious opinions should be tried. The criterion by which the Bible is to be interpreted is Jesus Christ."[4]

In seeing the mission of the church, the importance of the Bible cannot be overestimated. The Bible tells us who we are and what we are to do. It makes clear that the ultimate authority is Christ. It helps us understand the lordship of Christ over the church. Indeed, the church's mission is inscribed in Holy Scripture (Matt. 28:18-20). For guidelines for understanding the mission of the church, we must turn to the Bible.

The Bible is central to understanding the mission of the church because it is authoritative. "It finds man, searches him, makes him realize his need of spiritual help. If God speaks to man, he must speak in the tones of authority. He is not simply offering to man advice on spiritual matters which man may accept or reject as a matter of indifference. He speaks about man's sin, his salvation and destiny, in tones that are authoritative. There is a moral imperative in the message. Men talk today of a democratic God as if God were one of the common herd and as if his voice had no more authority than that of any other member of the mob. The Bible knows no such God. The God of the Bible is a God of holiness who speaks to man by the way of command."[5]

If the Bible is the authoritative source of our mission—and it is—then we not only must see that mission, but must get on with it.

THE IMPORTANCE OF PEOPLE IN THE
MISSION OF THE CHURCH

The mission of a church is to people. People are lost now. They need salvation now. Saved people need to grow. We must never forget that the work of the church has always been done on Christ's behalf to individuals, to persons.

No matter how scholarly our ideas or concepts, they are "sounding brass and tinkling cymbals" unless they become meshed with the hearts of the people. The goal of our proclamation, witness, and ministry is to reach out to persons; to reach out on behalf of our Lord to the teeming masses of bewildered, frightened, hurt, confused, anxious, and lonely people. Our mission is *for* Christ, *in* love, and *to* persons.

It will help us if we can see people as our Lord saw them. When he saw the multitudes, "He felt compassion for them, because they were distressed and downcast like sheep without a shepherd" (Matt. 9:36, NASB). To see them as Jesus saw them, we must see them as individuals; because he saw not a herd, but a

group of individuals, each with unique hurts and needs. He cared for individuals as a shepherd would care for one sheep (Luke 15). Jesus wept over the multitudes but he knew, loved, and ministered to individual needs.

The New Testament tells us:

- Nicodemus came by night to see Jesus and was told about the new birth (John 3:1-7).
- Blind Bartimaeus was seen and made to see (Mark 10:52).
- The woman at the well received the water of life from Jesus (John 4:14).
- A man with a withered hand was healed on the Sabbath (Mark 3:2).
- The leper who came alone to Jesus was cleansed (Mark 1:41).
- A woman who had a twelve-year hemorrhage was healed at the touch of his cloak (Mark 5:29).
- A paralytic who came to Jesus through the roof of a house was made to walk (Mark 2:1-4).
- The blind man who sat at the gate of the Temple received his sight (John 9).
- A man suffering from deafness and a speech impediment was made to hear and speak clearly (Mark 7:31-36).

Yes, our Lord took time for the rich and the poor, the respected and the outcast, the lovely and the unlovely, the sick and the well. He took time for the old and the young. Once he took a little child in his arms and stood in the midst of his disciples and said, "Whoever receives one child like this in My name is receiving Me" (Matt. 9:37, NASB).

Everything about our Lord's ministry, as well as his death and resurrection, reveals his great love and concern for persons.

RELATIONSHIP OF THE SUNDAY SCHOOL AND THE MISSION OF THE CHURCH

Because of the nature and mission of a church revealed in the Scriptures, and because of the centrality of the Bible in Sunday

School, the Sunday School is at the heart of the mission of the church. It is central—not a side issue; it is major—not minor. The Sunday School is, in fact, a force of great potential impact. There are more than 35,000 Sunday Schools with over 7.3 million persons enrolled. There are more than one million church-elected workers in the Sunday Schools. Envision the impact of such a force!

Tasks come directly to a Sunday School from the mission of the church: the tasks of reaching people and involving them in Bible study; the tasks of worshiping, witnessing, and winning persons to Christ and involving them in a ministry of loving, caring, and growing.

Since a Sunday School's tasks are given it by the church, a Sunday School can be thought of as a church reaching people and enrolling them in Bible study, as a church teaching the Word of God and witnessing to persons who need Jesus Christ as Savior. The Sunday School can be viewed as a church helping Christians grow through Bible knowledge and minister to others in his name.

It is my deep conviction that the Sunday School is well-equipped to serve as the major outreach organization of a church. I believe this for several reasons:

• One of the tasks of the Sunday School is to witness and to seek to bring persons to know and accept Christ as Savior and Lord. Witnessing is at the heart of the church's mission. The Sunday School through the years has shared the good news. The Sunday Schools of Southern Baptist churches have been used mightily in carrying out the mission of the church. The voices of Van Ness, Burroughs, Frost, Spilman, Flake, Barnette, and Washburn echo through the years the strong evangelistic concern for people. May it ever be so!

• The textbook of the Sunday School is the Bible. The Bible points the way to salvation and to the Christian life. Nothing else will suffice to meet man's deepest needs.

• The Sunday School is church centered. Our Lord gave his

commission to his church—no one else has this task. The Sunday School derives its mission from the church.

• The Sunday School has the largest membership of any organization. There are more persons enrolled in Sunday School; hence, a potentially large force to assist the church in its mission.

• It has the greatest potential constituency. Sunday School is for the youngest baby, for children of all ages, for youth and all adults—married or single. It is especially effective in reaching out to all members of all families.

• When the Sunday School is used as the outreach organization, there is less overlapping and duplication in efforts. The organization already exists. Churches need simply to train the teams they have and send them out to carry out the mission of our Lord.

• The Sunday School meets fifty-two weeks a year. It is not an "off-and-on" organization. It takes no vacation; it does not disband nor cut back in the summer. It is solid and stable. Throughout Southern Baptist history, the Sunday School has remained viable and alive—in good times and in bad.

• The Sunday School has the largest number of workers. Where else will you find one million workers with their task clearly defined?

• It is organized for outreach, for witnessing, for Bible study, and for ministering. The structure is there. The people are available. In fact, the assigning of a small group of persons to one worker is the genius of Sunday School outreach, witness, and ministry. The Spirit empowers.

With all of my heart, I believe that the Sunday School has its greatest days of outreach and ministry before it. Never have there been more lost persons. Never has the need to be on Christ's mission been more urgent. We must be aggressive in our pursuit of our Lord's objectives. Let us train the workers. Let us equip the members. Let us see our primary mission with twenty-twenty vision, and let us get on with it. We must not hesitate. We must not argue and bicker. We must move out. And, as we go, let us witness, share, and tell, asking God for his power. Let us ask him to make us aware and open to his Holy Spirit for leadership and for power. As we do this, we remember the last words of our Lord's commission, "I am with you always, even to the end of the age" (Matt. 28:20, NASB).

The remainder of this book will be an effort to interpret, lead to understanding, and delineate the work of the Sunday School.

[1]Herschel H. Hobbs, *The Baptist Faith and Message* (Nashville: Convention Press, 1971), p. 75.
[2]Ibid., p. 127.
[3]J. Clyde Turner, *These Things We Believe* (Nashville: Convention Press, 1956) p. 107.
[4]*The Baptist Faith and Message*, p. 74.
[5]W. T. Conner, *Christian Doctrine* (Nashville: Broadman Press, 1937) pp. 41-42.

Chapter 2

The Sunday School Is . . . Helping the Church Fulfill Its Mission

"He it is whom we proclaim. We admonish everyone without distinction, we instruct everyone in all the ways of wisdom, so as to present each one of you as a mature member of Christ's body" (Col. 1:28, NEB).

The church has a mission, and the Sunday School is a vital part of that mission. In the areas where it does its work, the Sunday School is the church fulfilling its mission. The history of the Sunday School movement will indicate the strength of the involvement of the Sunday School in the total mission of the church.

HISTORICAL DEVELOPMENT OF THE SUNDAY SCHOOL
Early Period (Before 1896)—Robert Raikes

Although he might not have started the first Sunday School, the man generally credited for getting the Sunday School movement going was the publisher of the *Gloucester Journal*, Robert Raikes. It was in 1780 that Raikes launched his "ragged school" in Sootey Alley. He sought to help poor children in his community by teaching them reading, writing, and religion. Six years later there were said to be 200,000 children attending Sunday Schools in England.

William Fox, a layman in a Baptist church in Clapton, England, became deeply interested in Raikes' Sunday Schools; and, in 1785, Fox was instrumental in forming the organization of the

Sunday School Union. His aim was to teach children to read the Bible. A fellow Baptist expressed the hope that Fox would confine the society to his own denomination. Fox replied, "I shall not be contented, Sir, until every person in the world is able to read the Bible."[1]

Some historians believe that the first Sunday School in America was established in the home of William Elliott, in Accomac County, Virginia, in 1785. If so, it is interesting to note that the "Sunday School movement and the United States of America were born together."[2]

In the latter part of the eighteenth century and the first part of the nineteenth Sunday Schools grew rapidly in various sections of the country. They were not church schools, however, as we know them today. While they were led by laymen, most often they were not a part of the organized work of the churches.

The first known Baptist Sunday School in the South was organized by 1803 by the Second Baptist Church in Baltimore, Maryland. It is claimed that "this school was distinctive in having religious instruction as its sole objective, and it may have been the first denominational Sunday school."[3]

During the first part of the nineteenth century, there were local Sunday School unions located mainly in the New England area. It was the Sunday School Union, organized in 1824, that gave Sunday School work a national scope. Over a fifty-year period, 1824-74, the Sunday School Union organized more than 60,000 Sunday Schools, many of which became churches. Numbered among the active supporters were men like Frances Scott Key, Daniel Webster, and Lyman Beecher.[4]

In 1845 a significant action was taken that deeply affected the Sunday School movement. In that year the Southern Baptist Convention was founded. The first Sunday School Board was formed in 1863; but, ten years later, it was merged with the Domestic and Indian Mission Board. In 1891, the present Sunday School Board was established in Nashville, Tennessee, with James M. Frost as its first secretary.

B. W. Spilman Period (1896 through 1920)

B. W. Spilman exerted great influence on Southern Baptist Sunday School work in his day. He was a pioneer Sunday School field worker in North Carolina and was the first Sunday School secretary among Southern Baptists. In 1901 he became the first field secretary of the Sunday School Board. He was the founder of Ridgecrest Baptist Assembly in 1907 and served consecutively as manager, general secretary, and president until 1933.

Spilman encouraged the seminaries to begin courses in religious education. He initiated teacher training and in 1902 wrote the first study course book, *Normal Studies for Sunday School Workers*. In 1941 he retired from the Sunday School Board. He richly deserved the title "The Sunday School Man."

Arthur Flake Period (1920 through 1943)

The Arthur Flake period is a monument to what God can do through the commitment and dedication of one person. Arthur Flake, born in Fayette County, Texas, had vision, clarity of thought, singleness of purpose, and abundant energy. He literally changed the face of his denomination.

Sometime after his conversion, he became superintendent of the Baptist Sunday School in Winona, Mississippi. He built it so successfully that he was sought widely for advice on building a Sunday School. In 1909 he became a Sunday School field worker. He told the world how to build a Sunday School:

1. Know your possibilities.
2. Enlarge the organization.
3. Provide the space.
4. Enlist and train the workers.
5. Go after the people.

Perhaps the best word to describe Arthur Flake is "pioneer." Nearly everything he did was new. It had not been done before. Among his significant achievements are the following: (1) the enlargement campaign, (2) the five-step formula for building a Sunday School, (3) *The Sunday School Builder* (of which he was editor from 1920 to 1936), (4) Sunday School clinics, (5) Standards of Excellence, (6) the Six Point Record System, (7) the church library movement, (8) weekly workers' meetings, (9) grading, (10) multiplication of units, and (11) the associational Sunday School organization.

He was the author of the following books:

Building a Standard Sunday School (1922)

Sunday School Officers and Their Work (1923)

Young People's and Adult Departments (1925)

The Sunday School Secretary and the Six Point Record System (co-author, Emma Noland) (1925)

The True Functions of the Sunday School (1930)

The Sunday School and the Church Budget (1931)

Life at Eighty As I See It (1944)

Flake's crowning work was the establishment and development of the Department of Sunday School Administration at the Sunday School Board in 1920. There were no guideposts, no textbooks, no literature, and no plans to follow. Vision, wisdom, courage, and energy were needed, and God provided all of these things in this remarkable man.

Even in retirement, Flake formulated a plan to memorize the Scripture by chapters and prayed for all phases of Southern Baptist life. This pioneer giant who said "it takes work to build a Sunday School" did indeed leave deep marks that affect Sunday School even to this day.

J. N. Barnette Period (1943 through 1957)

The next "flaming spirit" in Sunday School work was a school teacher in North Carolina. J. N. Barnette became a Christian in Double Springs Baptist Church of Shelby, North Carolina. Later, he led that church to have a Standard Sunday School and then to achieve the Advanced Standard. At age thirty-four he became the associate Sunday School secretary for North Carolina and gained Convention-wide recognition.

In 1927 J. N. Barnette became assistant to Arthur Flake in the

Arthur Flake (left) with I. J. Van Ness, corresponding
(executive) secretary of the Sunday School Board

Department of Sunday School Administration at the Sunday School Board. It is significant that he was first assigned to rural Sunday School work. In 1936 he became Sunday School promotional chairman of the Five Year Program, an emphasis on the association as a channel through which methods and resources of the Sunday School Board could be made available to every church.

In 1943 Dr. Barnette became secretary of the Sunday School Department. From 1943 to 1957 the Sunday School enrollment grew from 3,188,341 to 6,827,713, or a net of nearly four million.

J. N. Barnette was interested in the enlargement of the enrollment in Sunday Schools but he also was deeply concerned about winning lost persons to Christ. He said, "The winning of the lost to Christ is the most important work Southern Baptists have to do, and the Sunday School is one of the most effective means the church has for their first business." The impact of Barnette's influence was widely and deeply felt in Southern Baptist Sunday Schools.

Dr. Barnette was the author of the following books:

Associational Sunday School Work (1933)
A Church Using Its Sunday School (1937)
The Place of the Sunday School in Evangelism (1945)
The Pull of the People (1953)
One to Eight (1954)

A. V. Washburn Period (1957 through 1978)

The man who followed J. N. Barnette as Sunday School secretary came from Barnette's home church, Double Springs Baptist Church at Shelby, North Carolina. Converted at age nine, A. V. Washburn began teaching a Sunday School class at age sixteen.

In 1933, at age twenty-one, he became superintendent of Young People's work at the Sunday School Board. Some of the milestones in Washburn's life are as follows:

1943-46—Served in US Navy.
1946—Became secretary of teaching and training in the Sun-

day School Department.

1955—Wrote *Young People in the Sunday School.*

1957—Became secretary of the Sunday School Department and editor of *The Sunday School Builder.*

1960—Wrote *Outreach for the Unreached.* (He had been with Barnette during growth years.)

1966—Led in development of the Life and Work Curriculum.

1969—Co-authored (with Melva Cook) *Administering the Bible Teaching Program of a Church.*

1974—Co-authored (with James Fitch) *Reach Out to People.*

1975—Led in introduction of the ACTION plan of Sunday School enrollment.

A. V. Washburn had a deep and lasting influence on Southern Baptists. During the period that he served as secretary of teaching and training, leadership training reached its zenith. He served with the Sunday School Department in the golden years of growth and in the years when growth was slowed by the turbulent 60s and the changing 70s. In all those years, he was greatly loved by Southern Baptists. He always held high the banner of a Sunday School extending itself in loving concern to reach and minister to the masses. A. V. Washburn's influence remains strong and virile in this decade. His heart still beats for reaching people from all walks of life.

Certainly we are grateful for the historical roots of the Sunday School movement. We are grateful for that which God has done for the Sunday School through these great men. But the future is calling to us. Let us take a look at the specific tasks of the Sunday School in the year 1980 and beyond.

THE SUNDAY SCHOOL TASKS—THE CHURCH AT WORK

The mission of the church is indisputably clear. But how is it to be done? What is the strategy? It is precisely at this point that the Sunday School comes into clear focus. For the tasks of the Sunday School stem directly from the mission of the church. These tasks of the Sunday School are vital in helping the church carry out the

Great Commission.

Reach People for Bible Study

Simply stated this task involves leading persons to enroll and participate in Bible study. Certainly not all persons who are invited will enroll in Bible study; but there are thousands, even millions, who will. That is what the reaching task is all about. Most folks are not going to do much Bible study unless they are enrolled in a regular, systematic study of the Word. That is certainly not to say that Sunday Bible study is all the Bible study needed. Unfortunately, however, Sunday Bible study is far more than most persons in our nation now receive. The first task of the Sunday School is clear: Enroll countless thousands of persons in Bible study.

Through planned visitation and outreach programs, the Sunday School reaches out. The members—through worship opportunities, family relationships, and other contacts—are to be constantly alert and aware of opportunities to reach people for Bible study. Prospects should be enrolled in a class that faithfully studies the Bible week by week.

The Sunday School reaches out to all people. No one is left out. Provisions are made for all ages. Bible study should be provided for each member of the family regardless of condition.

For instance, handicapped persons should be provided for in the Sunday School. It is a sobering fact to realize that each year in the United States more than 126,000 children are born retarded. One out of every ten families in this country face unique problems related to mentally retarded children. Many children are born with physical handicaps, while others become physically handicapped later in life. These persons will need special provisions to make it possible for them to attend Bible study. A New Testament church has a commitment to reach all persons for Bible study.

A Sunday School should be trying to enroll all unenrolled persons. Special efforts need to be made, however, to enroll lost persons. It is a sad and tragic fact that there are few unsaved persons enrolled in the Sunday Schools today. Yet, the Bible and the Bible alone reveals the way to be saved. A Sunday School class or department is simply not fulfilling its purpose if it is not finding, cultivating, loving, and enrolling persons who are not Christians. Whatever else it may be doing, however good the fellowship of a class or department may be, if the group fails to enroll lost persons, it fails in one of its primary tasks.

Enroll the church members in Bible study. Some people are saved, join the church, and never enroll in Sunday School. How sad! Some are saved, join the church and Sunday School, and then drop out of one or both. This, too, is sad. There are more than thirteen million members of Southern Baptist churches. There are 7.3 million enrolled in Sunday School, of whom some 1.5 million—primarily preschoolers and children—are not church members. While 3.8 million members are nonresident, there still is an equal number of resident members not enrolled. What an opportunity! What a responsibility!

Teach the Bible

The Bible is the textbook of the Sunday School. While other lessons helps are used in preparation, it is the Bible that is studied; the written revelation of God is the Sunday School curriculum. We have a clear-cut and positive call to teach the Bible to the members and prospects of the Sunday School. Young and old, rich and poor, educated and uneducated—everyone can profit from a diligent, regular study of the Bible. Every person needs to study the Bible.

Teaching Bible content is essential. Content should not be neglected, pushed aside, taken lightly. Teaching content, however, is not enough. Application of the truths revealed in the content by learners to their activities and relationships must be crystal clear. The Bible is not an ancient book written to speak only to people who lived 2000 years ago. The Bible is a contemporary book. It is for us, today. It is for life here and now. Teaching is not the only purpose of the Sunday School, but we must never get away from a study of the sacred Word. Sunday School leaders today affirm that a major purpose of the Sunday School is to teach the Bible and all of its meaning to life.

Witness to Persons About Christ and Lead Them into Church Membership

The Sunday School cannot stop with enrolling persons in Bible study. Nor may it stop with teaching the Bible to those enrolled. Another purpose is to involve workers and members in introducing persons to Jesus and leading them to a personal faith relationship with Christ. When persons are discovered, enrolled, and involved in Bible study, when they are in warm fellowship with other class members, it is logical and natural that they be introduced to Jesus. It is not enough to live a Christian witness. We also must share a verbal witness about Christ and seek to lead lost persons to Christ. Personal evangelism is a clear and direct purpose of the Sunday School.

Neither must we stop when we have won persons to Christ. It is essential that those who become Christians follow the Lord in scriptural baptism and unite with a church. There is no church growth until the saved persons become members of the church. It is a matter of logic, common sense, and simple obedience (John 14:15). Jesus loved the church and gave himself for it. Redeemed persons will not look with disdain or disinterest on the church. They will want to be a part of it.

Minister to Sunday School Members and Non-Members

When lost persons are reached and enrolled in Bible study; when they are won to Christ and become a part of a Bible class and a New Testament church, then they can begin to grow, to worship and mature, to witness, and to minister to others. They are taught what it means to be followers of Christ. When we follow Christ in ministering to others, we are truly doing Christ's work in the world.

A Sunday School class that ministers to its members and prospects is meeting one of the basic needs that every human being has—the need of belonging. Fellowship, love, and caring should be an integral part of every Bible class.

Lead Members to Worship

Worship is a vital part of the life of a growing Christian. A Sunday School class should be vitally concerned about the participation of its members in public and private worship.

Certainly nothing can take the place of a congregational worship service. Nor should it. We are clearly taught the significance of worship in both Testaments. The writer to the Hebrews wrote, "Not forsaking our own assembling together, as is the habit of some but encouraging one another" (10:25, NASB). The psalmists' writings are full of references to the joy and blessings of worship. The Sunday School positively promotes the involvement of its members in regular congregational worship.

Not only is congregational worship essential, but so is individual worship. That is why the Sunday School member is encouraged daily to feed on the Word, to meditate, and to pray. Insight, understanding, and growth are inevitable by-products of the practice of daily devotions and Bible study.

There is no substitute, either, for family worship. Families will experience growth and strength as they read the Bible, discuss its meaning, and pray for strength. Such daily sharing will deepen understanding, help in problem solving, and strengthen family ties.

Interpret and Undergird the Work of the Church and the Denomination

The Sunday School has more members than any other church program organization. It has more leaders and prospects than any other. It has the organization and structure through which to do its work and much of the work of the church. Therefore, it is logical that it should interpret, support, and undergird all of the work of the church and the denomination.

When the church is involved in a revival, a stewardship campaign, a family life emphasis, or a Church Training event such as Baptist Doctrine Week, the Sunday School should give enthusiastic support and participation. It will strengthen the church and advance the cause of Christ when the Sunday School takes a strong and aggressive position in the church's worthy projects and goals. The Sunday School is not an organization apart; it is an organization that is a part of a church. Thus, every concern of a church deserves appropriate support from its Bible teaching program.

I HAVE A VISION

I love the church. I always have. Even so, I am not blind to its faults. It is not perfect. It couldn't be. Its members are sinners saved by grace. Nor is the church always right. It is not always true to its calling. But I love the church.

I was loved by Sunday School teachers before I was even conscious of their love. I felt that love as a little child and as a young lad. I experienced it as a youth and as a young adult. I have been inspired and have grown in Christ because of the church and the Sunday School. For twenty-five years I served as a staff member in churches. I am and have been richly blessed; so, with gratitude, I say that I love the church and I love the Sunday School.

Because of that love, I have a vision—a vision for the churches and Sunday Schools of the Southern Baptist Convention, a vision for each one of the more than 35,000 individual churches, and a vision for all of our church families and our Sunday School families.

I see more than 35,000 Sunday Schools across this magnificent land of ours with incredible potential. What does God want to do through us? What could he do through us if we were willing to be used? I see Sunday Schools multiplying and growing, enrolling new members and beginning new schools. We are more than

35,000 churches with more than 7 million members in Sunday School. Why not 70,000 churches with fourteen million in Sunday School or 140,000 with twenty-eight million? The clear purpose of Bold Mission Thrust is that every person in our nation and in the world hear the gospel in his/her own language. From Florida to Washington, from Hawaii to New York, from Texas to Michigan, from South Carolina to Arizona, from Puerto Rico to Alaska, I envision Sunday Schools penetrating a secular society with the gospel of Jesus Christ. I see our Lord changing the world through us who want his will done in our world. I have a vision of the multitudes enrolled in Sunday School classes and departments learning God's Word and its meaning in life. I see us learning to share, discuss, and grow together. I see us experiencing *koinonia* day by day, slowly but surely. I see us gaining new appreciation and insights into God's revelation to us and for us. I see his Word becoming real and vital in the lives of those who make up our fellowship and those who will become a part of it.

I see churches and Sunday Schools gaining a new appreciation of commitment to Christ's mission. I see Sunday School workers and members sharing Christ with the countless multitudes in our nation. I see Christ being shared in offices, businesses, schools, neighborhoods, and families. I see Sunday Schools doing regular evangelistic visitation—multitudes of persons coming to Christ. I have a vision of our Sunday Schools coming to a unique and life-changing understanding of ministry. I see us caring for and loving the hungry, outcast, and lonely persons for whom our Lord had great compassion.

What are your dreams for your church? Do you have a vision of what can happen in your church through its Sunday School? Do you have a dream for each class and each department? There is more to a vision than what you can see with the physical eye. A vision is something that is according to Webster, "seen otherwise than by ordinary sight." It is "unusual discernment or foresight"; it is "the act of perceiving mental images."

We don't need Webster, however, to know that visions are

seen with faith, the eyes of the soul. Concerning "the day of the Lord," about which Joel spoke and which Peter quoted at Pentecost, the prophet wrote that God would pour out his Spirit and "your sons and your daughters shall prophesy, your old men shall dream dreams, and your young men shall see visions" (Joel 2:28, RSV). God's Holy Spirit is the source and the interpreter of our dreams for the future. Let the Holy Spirit give you a vision of what your Sunday School can do and then empower you and your co-workers to bring the dream to reality!

---

[1]A. C. Underwood, *History of the English Baptists* (London: Carey Kingsgate Press, 1947) pp. 180-81.
[2]*Encyclopedia of Southern Baptists, Volume II* (Nashville: Broadman Press, 1958), p. 1316.
[3]Ibid., p. 1316.
[4]Ibid., p. 1316.

Part II

FOCUS ON PREPARATION

Chapter 3

The Sunday School Is . . . Organizing to Do the Work of the Church

"For it is under His direction that the whole body is perfectly adjusted and united by every joint that furnishes its supplies, and by the proper functioning of each particular part there is brought about the growing of the body for its building up in love" (Eph. 4:16, Williams).

The logical questions to ask at this point are: How will the mission of the church be done? Who will do it? So now we focus on preparation. In Part II, we ask: How do we organize in order to do the work of the church? How do we find and develop workers? Is planning ahead necessary for effective work?

Let us begin by asking a fundamental question. What is organization, anyway?

WHAT IS ORGANIZATION?

In the 1960s and, to some extent, the 1970s—we lived in an antiestablishment and antiorganization world. We often heard the comment, "He's just an organization man," or "She's just hung up on structure." "I'm not interested in organization, I'm interested in people," was another response. The inclination of many leaders was to de-emphasize organization and structure. In fact, some people almost apologized for using the word "organization," feeling that organization was not spiritual. It was not unusual to hear someone say, "I'm following the leadership of the Holy Spirit; so organization is just not needed."

With all of my heart, I want to follow the leadership of the Holy Spirit, but I am convinced that following his leadership does not preclude effective organization when our motivation and our aims are worthy and when we know what organization really is.

Simply put, organization involves having a task too big to perform by one person, dividing that task into reasonable parts, and asking persons to do parts of the whole. My father understood exactly what organization is. We lived on a few acres of land in times that were not easy for a father seeking to provide for his family. He supplemented his regular job with income derived from our small plot of ground. To get the work done, he divided it among himself and his five boys. I had cows to milk, corn to hoe, and a garden to weed. My other brothers had similar tasks. We knew exactly what those jobs were, and my father saw that we did them.

We five boys never once accused our father of being an "organization man." We knew that he knew exactly what he was doing. He was dividing the job into reasonable parts among his sons, instructing them in their assignment, and following up. There was nothing really complicated about that and it worked quite well.

Organization not only is practical, it also is scriptural. Remember the advice of Jethro to his son-in-law, Moses, as recorded in Exodus 18:13-27. While Jethro was visiting with Moses, Moses stood and judged the people from "morning till evening" (Ex. 18:13, RSV). Jethro saw what Moses was doing and asked, "Why do you sit alone and all the people stand about you from morning till evening?" (Ex. 18:14, RSV).

Moses replied that the people needed him. Jethro's practical and logical advice was to choose able men who would help Moses do the job. He would let these men be judges in all matters. They would bring only the greater matters to Moses. Moses accepted Jethro's advice and chose able men of Israel "and made them heads over the people, rulers of thousands, of hundreds, of fifties, and of tens" (Ex. 18:25, RSV). That was organization.

Paul, too, effectively used the principle of organization. Note his repeated visits back to the churches where he had left persons in positions of leadership. While the New Testament knew nothing of organization as we know it today, many of Paul's writings lay the foundation for organization; they contain the basics on which organization is built. His entire discussion concerning the body of Christ and its parts emphasizes interdependence, a principle on which organization relies (1 Cor. 12:12-26). (See Eph. 4:11; Acts 6:1-7; and 2 Tim. 2:2 for additional references containing basics for organization.)

Organization is not the power source in Sunday School. "Christ in us," the Holy Spirit, is the source of power. The organization is, rather, the vehicle that is used to carry out the Father's command. Understood, recognized, and used as such, organization can be an invaluable tool in fulfilling the mission of the church. The Sunday School is the church organized to fulfill the mission of the church.

WHAT IS TO BE ORGANIZED?

What is to be organized? The people who are members of the Sunday School are to be organized. The workers and the work are to be organized. Records are a story of the people and their work: thus, they, too, are a part of organization.

The People

We look first at the people. How will they be grouped and graded?

In 1970 Southern Baptist churches began to use a plan of grouping learners in church organizations that has served us well. We are continuing this organization plan in the 80s.

The Workers and the Work

While organization is a function of administration, it cannot exist by itself. Decisions on organization are made in the light of decisions on planning, staffing, directing, and evaluating the

THE GROUPING-GRADING PLAN

	Divisional Grouping Patterns			
	I.	II.**	III.**	IV.**
PRESCHOOL DIVISION	Birth-1 1* 2 3* 4 5*	B-1 1 2 3 4 5	B-1 1 2 3 4 5	B-1 1 2 3 4 5
CHILDREN'S DIVISION	6 (Grade 1) 7 (Grade 2)* 8 (Grade 3) 9 (Grade 4)* 10 (Grade 5) 11 (Grade 6)*	6 7* 8 9 10* 11	6 7 8 9 10 11	6 7 8 9 10 11
YOUTH DIVISION	12 (Grade 7) 13 (Grade 8)* 14 (Grade 9) 15 (Grade 10) 16 (Grade 11)* 17 (Grade 12)	12 13* 14 15 16* 17	12 13 14 15 16 17	12 13 14 15 16 17
ADULT DIVISION	18 (high school graduation) and up	18 (or high school graduation) Young Adult 29 30 Adult 59 (or retirement) 60 (or retirement) Senior Adult	18 (or high school graduation) Young Adult 1 2 29 30 Adult 1 2 59 (or retirement) 60 (or retirement) Senior Adult 1 2	18 (or high school graduation) Young Adult 1 2 3 4 29 30 Adult 1 2 3 4 59 (or retirement) 60 (or retirement) Senior Adult 1 2 3 4

*These ages will serve as the "focus group" for planning and offering curriculum materials to the churches for use with the pattern they select.

**Additional adult organization units should be added on the basis of possibilities in terms of classifications: college students, single or married persons, age.

work. All are valuable tools for accomplishing the objectives.

There is a limit to the number of persons a leader can effectively oversee. One fundamental function of organization is to divide the work into necessary activities and into segments small enough to be performed by, ideally, one person. This makes it necessary for organization structuring to be reviewed constantly in a church.

Sunday School work is done through three major structures. These are designated *classes, departments,* and *divisions.*

The first logical breakdown of the Sunday School into parts is the *division* structure. The term is used synonymously with "age-group" and does not imply that a division director is necessarily assigned. The grouping-grading plan, as seen in the accompanying chart, has four divisions: (1) Preschool: from birth through five years of age or school entrance; (2) Children's: ages six through eleven, or grades one through six; (3) Youth: ages twelve through seventeen, or grades seven through twelve; (4) Adult: ages eighteen, or high school graduation, up.

The *department* is the basic unit in the Preschool and Children's Divisions. In the Youth and Adult Divisions, the department is a combination of a number of classes into an administrative and teaching unit.

A *class* is the basic teaching and action unit of organization for Youth and Adult Divisions. The term "class" is not used in connection with Preschool and Children's Divisions.

Divisions, departments, and classes are determined by the number of possibilities for enrollment. Each unit of organization must contribute to the accomplishment of the objectives of the Sunday School. Each one must seek to achieve its own goals while, at the same time, working cooperatively with all other units.

Most Sunday Schools in their infancy, conducted an "assembly" with all Sunday School members present for the opening activity. Following this "assembly" period, members went to their respective meeting places for the remainder of the Sunday

School time. Since most Sunday Schools started small and often with limited facilities, this became the traditional approach to Sunday School in a small church.

The assembly period provided a rallying point for the members, a time for promotion and announcements, a time to introduce visitors; and a brief period for devotional or worship experience.

As the Sunday School grew and as Sunday School leaders learned more about their work, however, they moved toward a more departmentized organization.

This move usually was begun with a department for preschoolers. It was recognized that preschoolers could best be provided for during the total Sunday School period if they were in rooms especially provided for them and with workers who were prepared to help them with happy learning experiences.

The next move was to a department organization for children (grades 1-6). Even if there were only two or three children, it was felt that children could best learn by being in a room with a well-prepared teacher for the entire Sunday School period.

So today the old "class" Sunday School idea is disappearing and preschoolers and children are being taught Bible truths through activities and projects planned for them. Under this arrangement, the groupings are called "departments" instead of "classes."

With a department organization, Preschool and Children's workers can be present before the first child arrives and direct his activity from the moment he comes into the room.

In a small Sunday School, the youth and adults may continue with the assembly time for a while even though preschoolers and children have formed their departments. Such an assembly may continue with only one or two classes for youth and for adults. This can be a useful part of the Sunday morning Bible study experience. It should be noted, however, that youth leaders probably will prefer to meet their pupils for the total Sunday School time. It also is important to know that youth curriculum is planned for total-period teaching during the Sunday School time.

Youth leaders and adult leaders will come to the time when they want the total Sunday School period with their age group. When this time comes, a fully departmentized Sunday School can be organized.

For more information on organizing to meet the needs of all persons, see the discussion that follows and the age-group books in the "Basic Sunday School Work Series."

How Preschool Sunday School is organized.—Boys and girls from birth until they enter first grade are members of or prospects for the Preschool Division. Within this division, the Sunday School has one or more Preschool departments. Each separate room for preschoolers is considered a department room. The department is made up of the preschoolers enrolled in that age group and the workers in that department. Each department has a director and one or more teachers. A division director may be needed if there are several departments for preschoolers. See *Basic Preschool Work* for a description of the division director's job.

Meeting the needs of preschoolers is the first consideration when grouping Preschool departments in a church. Meeting the needs of a preschooler involves developing a sense of trust, which is essential in helping him feel secure. When he develops a sense of trust and security, he then can begin to accept learning opportunities made available to him at church. It is upon this foundation that the child's love of God develops.

Younger preschoolers (birth to two years of age) are grouped according to their physical development rather than by their chronological age. When a baby begins to crawl, he is moved to the Creeper department. As a creeper begins to walk, he is moved into the Toddler department. Middle preschoolers (two- and three-year-olds) and older preschoolers (four- and five-year-olds) are grouped according to the system used by the public schools in your area or the system your church uses for grouping other age groups. When possible, a church should move to a separate department for each age group (or developmental stage) in the Preschool Division. Teaching preschoolers usually is much easier and more effective when the age range in the department is small. Even a few preschoolers together in one room can have good learning experiences at church as teachers plan well to meet their needs.

The proper ratio of teachers to preschoolers is a key to effective work: babies through toddlers, one worker for every three children enrolled but no fewer than two workers in any department; two- through five-year-olds, one worker for every four children enrolled. The total potential enrollment in each department should not exceed the following. If enrollment does exceed this maximum, start a new department.

Age	Maximum Enrollment (Preschoolers)	Workers Needed
Babies	9	3
Creepers	9	3
Toddlers	9	3
Twos	12	3
Threes	16	4
Fours	16	4
Fives	16	4

Cradle Roll—one worker for every six to eight families

The smallest Sunday School, for a time, may find it necessary to have all preschoolers in one teaching unit (department) and may have only three to five members. When the enrollment reaches six or seven, and most of the preschool ages are represented, a new department can be started—one for younger preschoolers and one for older preschoolers. The younger department would include babies through two-year-olds, and the older department would include ages three through five.

With two departments, when the number of members enrolled in each department reaches eight to ten, an additional department may be started. The three departments then would be: younger preschoolers, birth through one year; middle preschoolers, ages two and three; and older preschoolers, ages four and five.

Basic needs of preschoolers are such that often one child will require the attention of a worker for a period of time; so it is preferable to have at least two workers in each department. As the enrollment increases, the member-worker ratios mentioned above should be maintained.

Additional help for organizing to reach preschoolers may be found in *Basic Preschool Work.*

How Children's Sunday School is organized.—All boys and girls in grades one through six, or six through eleven years of age, are in the Children's Division. Within this division, a church will have one or more departments.

The years from grade one through grade six bring dramatic changes in children. Sizes change. New skills are developed. Changed attitudes come into play. Compared to himself at age six, nearly any eleven-year-old seems an almost altogether different creature. For this reason, children in the Children's Division are best understood when the age span is broken into smaller segments: younger children (ages six and seven), middle children (ages eight and nine), and older children (ages ten and eleven). Children at these different levels have special characteristics. Some approaches useful at one level are relatively ineffective at another.

Possible groupings of children for Sunday School are identified in The Grouping-Grading Plan chart (p. 37). Factors influencing the number of Children's departments a church should have are number of children enrolled, number of prospects, department room or space available, leadership available, and equipment needed.

In some larger churches, more than one department of each age within the Children's Division may be needed. Three focus ages in the Foundation line of curriculum materials make the formation of at least three departments desirable.

In smaller churches, one department (grades one through six) may be adequate if space and leadership are limited and if the projected enrollment is less than ten. If space and workers are available, however, two departments—ages six through eight and nine through eleven—are highly desirable, regardless of small enrollment. While Foundation curriculum materials are effective in any Children's department, the Convention Uniform Children's curriculum materials provide a choice in situations where there are only one or two workers.

Workers needed within a Children's Sunday School department are a department director, an outreach leader, teacher(s), and a secretary (optional). When there is only one worker for a department, the worker assumes the role of teacher and is responsible for outreach activities. In a church that has four or more Children's departments, a division director may be needed. For a study of the duties of Children's Sunday School workers, see *Basic Children's Sunday School Work,* chapter 3.

How Youth Sunday School is organized.—The basic unit of organization in the Youth Division of the Sunday School is the class. The maximum enrollment in a Youth class should be ten to fifteen and the department enrollment should be in the range of forty to sixty youth. There should be at least one worker for every ten to fifteen youth. Grouping by classes is necessary to maintain consistency in the reaching, witnessing, and ministry areas of Youth Sunday School. A teacher can minister to ten or fifteen youth; but, if the number grows larger, then the requirement of the teacher is too great. Classes can be graded by sex or by age (grade in school).

The terms department/class and large group/small group are used in Youth Sunday School. Youth Sunday School is organized—using those terms—to help Youth workers meet the needs of their youth with a consistent *reaching organization* and an effective *teaching-learning process.*

Youth communicate in many ways that they like variety. Using various groupings, then, of large group/department and small group/class can work to our advantage in the teaching-learning process of Youth Sunday School. The use of total-period teaching allows a class and/or department to spend its entire time on Sunday morning in Bible study. (Total-period teaching simply means that all learning experiences planned for youth on Sunday morning are related to one Scripture passage and to one central or basic truth.)

Department/class organization provides an ongoing, established, consistent pupil-teacher relationship that is essential to meet the needs of youth.

Large/small group provides the variety of schedules and groupings and offers the flexibility that is necessary to keep youth involved in Bible study.

Department/class organizes people (youth and Youth workers) to reach out to, witness to, and minister to other youth during the week.

Large group/small group organizes people (youth and Youth workers) to participate in challenging Bible study sessions on Sunday morning.

A small Sunday School, with no more than six to eight youth, may have all grades, seven through twelve, in one class. When the enrollment reaches ten to fifteen, two classes may be organized, one for grades seven through nine and one for grades ten through twelve. These may operate as classes in a class-organized school or as a department.

Additional classes may be organized as the number of members increases. When a class, having multiple ages in it, reaches ten to fifteen, a new class could be organized. Several classes may be formed within the one department.

For more information on how to organize for effective Youth work, read the suggestions in *Basic Youth Sunday School Work,* chapter 4.

How Adult Sunday School is organized.—The Adult class is the basic unit for getting Adult Sunday School work accomplished. To be most effective, an Adult class probably should not have more than twenty-five members enrolled. In a small Sunday

School, the enrollment per class should be smaller so as to narrow the age span of a class.

The personnel in the class includes a teacher, a class outreach leader, a class activities leader, group leaders, a secretary, and members. For a list of duties of each class leader, see chapter 6 in *Basic Adult Sunday School Work*.

When the number of adults enrolled is large enough for two classes, an Adult department should be organized. Many small Sunday Schools may have two Adult classes, divided either between younger adults and older adults or between men and women. A department organization would strengthen the work of these classes.

In some churches with a large Adult enrollment, several departments may be needed. To enable leaders to do a more thorough job, no more than six classes should be assigned to any one department, with a department maximum enrollment of 125.

The department leadership team may include a department director, a department outreach leader, a department activities leader, and a department secretary. For a better look at suggested details of duties for department leaders, see chapter 6 in *Basic Adult Sunday School Work*.

When the number of departments grows, some churches use one more step in organization—the Adult Division, made up of several Adult departments. The Adult Division director works primarily through Adult department directors, assisting them in all facets of their work.

Provision also should be made for special groups of adults when the need exists. A church should consider providing departments for these groups: Homebound adults, young adults away, Sunday workers, the physically handicapped, language groups, college students, and single adults. Organizational guidelines for these special groups can be found in chapter 9 of *Basic Adult Sunday School Work*.

Organizing for special persons in Sunday School.—Every Sunday School has the challenge of providing for persons with special needs. These persons include the mentally retarded, blind or visually impaired persons; those who are deaf or hard-of-hearing; persons with other physical handicaps; and those for whom English is a second language. Every community has such people, many of them unreached for Bible study, Christ, or church membership.

Often the needs of special persons can be met through existing organizations. For instance, a special person sometimes can be included in a class or department by adding one person to work specifically with him. When church buildings are designed to remove architectural barriers, persons in wheelchairs can attend.

At times separate provision is needed for some handicapped persons. Good questions to ask when considering separate units for special persons include these:

- How well can the person's needs be met in an existing class or department?
- To what extent does the person's presence disrupt the functioning of the existing group?
- Is special curriculum or equipment needed to meet the needs of the person?

Organization required for separate provision corresponds closely to organization needed for regular classes and departments. The pupil-teacher ratio, however, usually needs to be lowered.

Can one Sunday School possibly provide Bible study for so many diverse groups? That depends upon (1) the number of qualified workers available or trainable and (2) the availability of suitable space and equipment. Special persons are the Sunday School's opportunity. How much a church desires to act on the opportunity probably will determine whether these provisions are made.

Organizing for special projects.—Short-term Bible teaching projects may be conducted at times other than Sunday to provide additional Bible study for Sunday School members and for persons who do not attend on Sunday. Curriculum for each of these projects is provided by the Sunday School Board. These projects serve as feeders to the church's regular Sunday School study. They also provide a rich area of outreach potential. These special projects offer unlimited possibilities of penetrating the 130-160 million unchurched people in our nation. Consider these possibilities:

- Church Vacation Bible School

Leadership requirements for VBS are a director; assistant directors, who serve as chairmen of various committees, as needed, such as refreshment and transportation; and a department director and teachers for each department, Preschool through Adult. The Sunday School grouping-grading plan and teacher-pupil ratio apply to church Vacation Bible School.

- Mission Vacation Bible School

Mission VBS is a five-day Bible study activity targeted to preschoolers, children, and youth who do not attend Sunday School. The organization is similar to church VBS. Mission schools often provide a nucleus of workers and members for starting a new Sunday School.

- Backyard Bible Clubs

These are mini Bible Schools for children ages six through eleven, conducted in backyards, carports, patios, or open areas in the community. They usually are held for one and a half hours a day for five days.

- January Bible Study

This is an additional Bible study activity for all ages. The Adult Bible study focuses on a book of the Bible, as does the Youth study. This has traditionally been called January Bible study, though many churches select another time for their studies. New Adult and Youth books and age-graded Bible study books and units are provided by the Sunday School Board for this Bible study. This activity can be especially successful in involving church members not in Sunday School as well as unchurched members of a community.

- Bible Conferences

A Bible Conference is a supplementary Bible study activity, involving adults and youth in a number of alternate Bible courses on Bible books or Bible themes. Often this conference is planned for the association with all churches participating. Special Bible study materials are provided for this project by the Sunday School Board. Such conferences also provide a great potential for involving unsaved persons in Bible study.

The Records

Sunday Schools can set up and maintain a record system and still not benefit from record keeping. People are the reason records are important. Records must be used—not just to *validate* keeping records but to *evaluate* the effectiveness of the Sunday School program with relation to its people. Keeping thorough, up-to-date, accurate records requires work but it is not just busy work. Keeping good records provides Sunday School leaders with practical, indispensable information about people. Records are of no value until they are used—with people in mind. Here are some ways to use your records. (See also the section on using records in outreach, chapter 8.)

Use records to evaluate.—By analyzing class, department, and school records over a period of time, leaders can note areas of advancement or decline. Records can indicate spiritual decline or indifference on the part of members. Thorough records can help leaders answer these questions: What has happened to Sunday School enrollment this year? What has happened to attendance? How does this year's attendance pattern compare with last year's record? How many adults are attending worship? Are members reading their Bibles daily? What persons are irregular in attendance? When did they begin to be irregular in attendance? Are members growing in their stewardship of money? Are members studying their lessons? Which departments are regularly contacting prospects and members? In which departments is visitation considered a priority? Are new members being enrolled regularly? Are unsaved members being added to the Sunday School rolls?

When leaders use records to answer questions about people, they see where people needs exist and can plan accordingly to bring about improvement where it is needed most. The Sunday School council depends heavily on people records to chart the course for the Bible teaching program. The outreach director can rely on the record system to tell him how effectively outreach leaders are involving members in penetrating the community with the gospel. If we are genuinely interested in reaching people and teaching them through the Word, we will make wise use of records.

Use records to motivate.—Records are motivational tools for members. As they check their own achievements—according to the points on either the Broadman Revised Sunday School Record System or the Broadman Sunday School Six Point Record System—they may be inwardly convinced of their need to improve in areas of spiritual discipline. And, as leaders review records with workers, the need for improvement becomes evident. Seeing a need is the point where motivation to improve can begin.

Use records to enable.—Records can be enabling tools. Accurate records provide leaders with direction in planning. Having the facts in hand adds validity to the concerns and efforts of leaders as they lead the Sunday School to accomplish its purpose. Records enable leaders to set priorities and goals with authority and confidence that they will help accomplish Sunday School tasks.

A list of record forms used in each age group appears under "Resources for Sunday School Work" in the back of this book.

HOW WILL THE ORGANIZATION BE MAINTAINED?

The Sunday School responds effectively to loving care and consistent attention. When its organization is "maintained," it grows in effectiveness. How will it be maintained?

By the Pastor's Leadership and Support

Concern and care for the organization begin with the pastor; *the pastor is the key.* No Sunday School can do its best without the pastor's guidance and concern. If the pastor believes in, works with, and supports the Sunday School, it has a greater chance of reaching, teaching, and winning persons to Christ. No one can take the pastor's place. He is the pastor of the Sunday School because he is pastor of the church. Of course, this in no way implies that he makes all the decisions or does all the work. It does mean that he sees the Sunday School as the outreach arm of the church, as the Bible teaching agency, and as the organization best equipped to carry out these tasks.

The pastor can demonstrate his leadership and support in several ways each week: (1) He can study records to determine whether each teaching unit is functioning and where worker vacancies exist. (2) He can walk through the building(s), evaluating present use of space and location of possible new units. (3) He can walk through the building on Sunday morning and observe in the various departments or he may visit Sunday School classes at different times. (4) He can attend and participate in the Sunday School council and weekly workers' meetings. (5) He can recognize Sunday School workers during the worship hour. (6) He can preach on the mission of the church and relate the place of the Sunday School to that mission. (7) He can attend various Sunday School department activities, such as fellowships, banquets, and retreats. (8) He can be involved in training Sunday School members in how to witness. (9) He can participate and lead out in planned visitation and witnessing through the Sunday School.

By a Functioning Sunday School Council

The Sunday School council exists for planning and evaluation. (See chapter 5 for makeup of the Sunday School council.) It does more than discuss vacancies and review the calendar. It sets goals and makes plans to reach them. The council should meet a minimum of once a month. In some churches, it meets each week in conjunction with the weekly workers' meeting.

Through Annual Promotion

Promotion recognizes the natural laws of growth and development and is a necessary factor in the normal, healthy growth of a Sunday School. To keep the Sunday School graded, proper classification and annual promotion are equally necessary. With age grading, the Sunday School avoids unnecessary competition among classes. With age grading, assignment of prospects becomes relatively simple.

Ten clear values of annual promotion can be cited:

1. Promotion provides for normal advancement through the natural stages of life.

2. Promotion encourages a person to adapt to changing conditions.

3. Promotion provides guidance and influence of a larger number of consecrated teachers.

4. Promotion creates new places of service for many class members.

5. Promotion brings fresh interest in prospects by reassigning them to new workers.

6. Promotion removes the vacuum in which cliques often develop.

7. Promotion brings new friends, new relationships.

8. Promotion brings new life.

9. Promotion means a "new beginning."

10. Promotion makes possible new growth.

Through Regular Reports to the Church

Regular reports produce better work since they offer recognition and encouragement to persons. The church may ask the Sunday School director or a staff member to report briefly each Sunday morning concerning the achievements of the Sunday School. Occasionally recognition for significant achievement is appropriate. A report board is helpful; it may be shown in the worship service or placed in a hall or entry way for all to see on leaving. Detailed reports may be given through the church weekly paper and may be studied at weekly workers' meeting. A Sunday School report should be part of the business meeting records of the church. Tell the people what is happening in and through the Sunday School.

Through Practice of the Team Concept

The Sunday School leadership is a team in the best sense of the word.

The pastor, the minister of education, other educational leaders (if a church has them), the Sunday School director, and all Sunday School leaders make up the team. They must plan together and pray together. They must work together. They must pull together and move together in the same direction. Harmony must be visibly present. Criticism must be avoided. Each team member must not be concerned about who gets the credit or the blame. Each must know that it is God who gets the glory for every victory won. The Sunday School team—committed, dedicated, and serving in love and harmony—can accomplish miracles through its ministry to and through people.

WHAT ARE SOME ORGANIZATION OPTIONS?

Frequently churches are confronted with situations calling for an organizational approach that may not reflect the recommended structures identified in *Basic Sunday School Work.* In such cases, some organizational options are needed for organizing in a small church, structuring teaching units in a middle-size church, adapting the organization for a large church, struggling with the basics in the inner city, living with limitations in a mission area, and altering plans to meet persons or groups of persons with special needs.

Guidelines for Considering Organization Options

When situations call for optional approaches, leaders have to decide how best to offer Bible learning experiences to the persons involved. It is not possible for specific suggestions to be offered for every situation. As consideration is given to proper organization, the overarching question to be asked is, What is the best grouping for maximum learning and outreach? Other questions, also, may arise: Are the *needs* of the individuals to be reached and taught of primary consideration? Has a definite *effort* to achieve recommended organization been attempted? Have the largest possible *number of leaders* been involved in the decision-making process? Has all available help from denominational resources been obtained? Are the proposed *methodologies* educationally sound? Has the *potential for crises* in such areas as enrollment, leadership, and space been fully examined? Have all possible means been used to *inform and orient workers* preceding the time changes or adjustments to be implemented?

Listed below are some special guidelines for specific situations:

1. Small church

a. Usually there should be at least one Preschool department, a Children's department, a Youth class, and one or perhaps two Adult classes with the second being a Young Adult class.

b. More than one leader is needed in a Preschool or Children's department.

2. Middle-size church

a. Decide whether enlisting division directors would contribute to an improved organizational plan rather than limiting staff to the number of department workers available.

b. Provide organization patterns that make room for new groups of single adults, language groups, and persons with special needs.

c. Remain sensitive to changing enrollment pattern in order to maintain a flexible organization, which allows for easy starting of new teaching units.

3. Large church

a. Division directors and/or multiple paid staff members

usually have overall supervision of the age division.

b. Greeters, classification secretaries, parking lot monitors, media center personnel, and others are required for operating a large Sunday School.

c. The larger the enrollment, the greater the number of options available. For example, alternate Bible studies for certain groups of persons who to date have chosen not to be involved may reach some of them. Advanced leadership training classes on Sunday morning may be scheduled and may play an important role in the total Sunday School.

d. Because of the largeness of the organization, special efforts must be made to help members in the teaching units relate to and be a part of the larger fellowship.

4. Inner-city church

a. Organization may be heavily weighted with senior adults or neighborhood children, while including comparatively few youth and young adults.

b. Where insufficient number of leaders exists, the organization often has a higher ratio of members to workers. Strong efforts should be made to change this situation.

c. Space and facilities (sometimes too much and too old) may require adjustments.

d. There may be a need to start another Sunday School in the main building or a nearby building for a different socio-economic group not being reached by the church. Language groups offer a great potential for new Sunday Schools.

e. Schedules and meeting times may need to be adjusted to the type of community involved.

5. Mission area

a. Mission situations may involve groups with wide age spans, which sometimes may even cross division lines. This fact, as well as the high ratio of members to teachers and sometimes undesirable and inadequate meeting places, often demand adjustments.

b. In some cases, age divisions may have to meet at different times because of space or leadership problems.

c. Adults often are not present with their children. This fact may call for special attention to children during worship services.

d. Inexperienced teachers frequently are thrust into leadership roles without adequate training or lesson course helps. They may become discouraged.

TIMELESS FORMULA FOR SUNDAY SCHOOL ORGANIZATION

We have looked at the integral parts of Sunday School organization and have indicated how the Sunday School should be put together to do the most effective job possible in reaching people and teaching them the Bible. Years ago, a basic formula was suggested for administering a reaching and teaching Sunday School. Southern Baptist churches have learned through the years of experience that these basic, practical, and time-proven steps should be taken in building a Sunday School.

While portions of these steps are covered in various chapters of this book, the basic description best fits in this chapter.

Southern Baptists through the years have known these steps as Flake's Formula. Arthur Flake identified laws of Sunday School growth, which he applied in five steps. The principles have appeared from time to time, clothed in a variety of terms. They do require updated methodologies but the principles have stood the test of time.

Step 1.—Know your possibilities. The possibilities include two groups of people: (1) those already enrolled in Sunday School, and (2) those not enrolled who are possibilities. Unenrolled possibilities for Sunday School include church members not enrolled in Sunday School, all persons in a community or city not enrolled in any Sunday School and not members of any church, all persons who prefer to attend a Baptist Sunday School, and all persons who have no preference.

Actually, a church is as much responsible for one group as another. The simple fact is that a Sunday School is responsible for reaching the saved and the lost. It must know who these persons are. The name, address, and date of birth make it possible to assign every possiblity to some class or department of the Sunday School. A religious census or survey remains one of the best ways to discover the possibilities.

Step 2.—Enlarge the organization, or provide the right organization. This step simply means that an adequate number of the right size classes and departments must be provided in order to reach the possibilities. In most cases, this will mean an enlargement of the present organization. New classes and departments will need to be created. In this day of bold reaching and teaching—bold new enlargement is critical now!

Step 3.—Provide the space. Each existing and new class or department will need adequate space. Sunday School leaders should do a space study to determine what is essential. If a church fails to provide needed space, even though all else has been done, it is hardly possible to have substantial growth. That is not to say that growth is *produced* by space, *it is not*—but growth is *made possible* by the provision of space.

The kind and quality of the space also is important. It has to do with growth. The proper provision of space also determines the organization possible. If balanced provision has been made, the Sunday School has the possibility of balance in reaching and teaching. If one age group or segment has been neglected, the Sunday School reflects that fact. That is what is meant by the statement, "The Sunday School takes the shape of the building."

Step 4.—Enlist and train workers. If a Sunday School knows its possibilities, enlarges the organization, and provides the space, it will have little value unless sufficient, properly enlisted, and adequately trained workers are provided. Additional trained workers obviously are needed for replacement and expansion. Present workers need to improve in reaching and teaching. Hence, a fifty-two-weeks-a-year program of enlistment and training is essential. See chapter 4 for detailed discussion of enlistment and training.

Step 5.—Go after the people. If there is a "most important" step in these five steps, it is this one. All four previous steps may be followed, but if the workers and members do not go, do not visit, do not witness, and do not minister, the Sunday School will become stagnant. It will turn inward. It will become "maintenance" conscious. It will become protective, conservative, and probably negative—or at least indifferent.

The church must go. The Sunday School must go. It must go continually. It must go regularly, systematically. It must go joyfully.

The Sunday School must go to the absentees, to the prospects, to the indifferent, and to the unsaved. The Sunday School members and leaders must go in personal, daily witness in their circles of influence. They must go in regularly weekly planned visitation. Every Sunday School ought to have definite weekly visitation. The Sunday School must go to all people at all times.

Chapter 4

The Sunday School Is . . . Finding and Developing Workers

"Why is it that he gives us these special abilities to do certain things best? It is that God's people will be equipped to do better work for him, building up the church, the body of Christ, to a position of strength and maturity" (Eph. 4:12, TLB).

The Scriptures clearly teach that spiritual gifts are given to each member of the body of Christ. No one is left out. Each Christian does have a gift and should use it. Peter's writing is clear: "As each has received a gift, employ it for one another, as good stewards of God's varied grace" (1 Pet. 4:10, RSV).

GIFTS ARE GIVEN

Paul told Timothy: "Do not neglect the gift you have. . . . Practice these duties, devote yourself to them, so that all may see your progress" (1 Tim. 4:14-15, RSV).

There is not total agreement on the listing of these gifts as reported especially in 1 Corinthians 12:1-3; Romans 12:3-8; and Ephesians 4:11. Whatever the gifts, it is abundantly clear that they are to be used in the work of the church (1 Pet. 4:10; 1 Tim. 4:14). They were not given to be put on the shelf. Gifts not used and developed are an affront to the giver and a grievous loss to the body of Christ, his church. There are enough gifts given to do the work of the church, if each member performs his gift.

ROLE OF THE WORKER IDENTIFIED
Sunday School Workers Are Volunteers
A beautiful truth to be remembered is that Sunday School workers are volunteers. They are not paid in money or any other material way. Their rewards are measured through a deep and abiding sense of satisfaction derived from doing God's will. Often a Sunday School worker has said, "You couldn't pay me to do what I do." That is exactly right. Sunday School workers serve because they feel called; Sunday School workers serve because they want to do God's will.

Sunday School Workers Are Qualified
Every member of the body has gifts that can be used in various Sunday School responsibilities, which require those gifts. Let us observe the qualities and characteristics of a Sunday School leader calling for gifts from God. Can these be identified?

The Sunday School worker has a sense of calling.—Any disciple can know that God calls him to his task. The apostle Paul surely felt God's calling. He wrote to the Romans, "Paul, a bond-servant of Christ Jesus, called as an apostle" (Rom. 1:1, NASB). And to the Corinthians, "Paul an apostle of Christ Jesus by the will of God" (2 Cor. 1:1, NASB). Then, to Timothy, "Paul, an apostle of Christ Jesus according to the commandment of God our Savior" (1 Tim. 1:1, NASB).

For twenty-five years I enlisted Sunday School workers for service in the local church. It was my practice to ask, "Will you pray and ask God's guidance? Please do not accept or decline until you have asked him." I followed this practice because I believe that Sunday School workers can know God's call.

The Sunday School worker understands the task.—The effective Sunday School worker knows that he or she has a high and holy task because the task is from God. And the Sunday School worker understands that the basic task is to "make disciples" (Matt. 28:19, NASB): to lead persons to a personal faith in Jesus Christ. The Sunday School worker knows further that his task is "teaching them to observe" (Matt. 28:20); to lead the believers to grow in the grace, knowledge, and life of our Lord Jesus. The Sunday School worker understands the clear message of John 20:21: "as my Father hath sent me, even so send I you." The Sunday School worker understands Acts 1:8, NASB, "You shall be My witnesses." A clear understanding of the task is always a prerequisite to effective work.

The Sunday School worker is committed to the task.—It is one thing to know what the task is; it is quite another to bring commitment to it. The Sunday School worker does exactly that. He or she identifies with Paul in his commitment to the goal: "One thing I do: forgetting what lies behind and straining forward to what lies ahead, I press on toward the goal" (Phil. 3:13-14, RSV).

The Sunday School worker has integrity and self-understanding.—You have integrity when you are what you appear to be. You have integrity when your life reflects what you say. Integrity is an indispensable quality of the Sunday School worker. Character, honesty, and truthfulness are the foundation stones of integrity. The apostle Paul wrote, "We are so glad that we can say with utter honesty that in all our dealings we have been pure and sincere" (2 Cor. 1:12, TLB). Integrity is absolutely essential. One may teach a *little* by what he *says, more* by what he *does,* but *most* by what he *is.* Integrity is important because Christian truths are better understood when they are demonstrated in day-to-day living. They are more caught than taught.

The Sunday School worker knows who he is. He has some definite goals in life. He knows that there is always struggle and usually no easy answers. He can accept criticism, receive advice, and listen to others. He has a degree of security because he knows and understands himself.

The Sunday School worker prepares.—No one can teach Scripture effectively without preparation—physical, mental, and spiritual. The Sunday School teacher should be physically prepared. That is to say, he must do his best to keep his body in good condition. Though Paul was writing to the Corinthians about moral conduct, he gave us an admonition appropriate for all of life: "Do you not know that your body is a temple of the Holy Spirit who is in you, whom you have from God and that you are not your own? For you have been bought with a price" (1 Cor. 6:19-20, NASB). Getting adequate rest in order to be fresh when teaching is an example of applying this Scripture passage to our personal life-style.

Mental preparation means studying the Scripture and seeking understanding and application from various commentaries and other books and resources. Nothing will substitute for studying God's Word in order to learn from it and to know its meaning. Learning does not happen by osmosis.

Preparation also involves spiritual preparation. Even though physical and mental processes have been undertaken, one can miss the mark if he fails prayerfully to seek the guidance and leadership of the Holy Spirit. Nothing substitutes for prayer. Physical, mental, and spiritual preparation are vital to the effectiveness of the Christian leader.

The Sunday School worker is enthusiastic.—The word "enthusiasm" actually comes from the Greek word *entheos*, meaning inspired by God. Most effective leaders are enthusiasts. In Proverbs we read, "A joyful heart is good medicine, but a broken spirit dries up the bones" (Prov. 17:22, NASB). Enthusiasm in Bible teaching must come through with a clear message. Paul wrote: "If the man who plays the bugle does not sound a clear call, who will prepare for battle?" (1 Cor. 14:8, GNB). The Bible is an exciting book with fantastic ideas for making life exciting; it needs to be taught clearly by enthusiastic people.

The Sunday School worker delegates.—The worker shares the load. He divides the task, involves the people. He knows that he cannot do it all; so he makes use of the department and class organizations. Organization is to be used; it is not decorative. When one has a job too big to do by himself, what should he do? Divide it up into reasonable parts and assign it to appropriate and willing persons. That is delegation; that is organization. Remember the advice that Moses received from Jethro, his father-in-law. Divide the task. Delegate responsibilities. It is better for a Sunday School worker to enlist ten persons than to do the work of ten.

The Sunday School worker is faithful.—To the Corinthians, Paul wrote, "Therefore, my beloved brethren, be steadfast, immovable, always abounding in the work of the Lord, knowing that your toil is not in vain in the Lord" (1 Cor. 15:58, NASB).

To the young preacher, Timothy, Paul wrote: "But you be sober in all things, endure hardship, do the work of an evangelist, fulfill your ministry. For I am already being poured out as a drink offering, and the time of my departure has come. I have fought the good fight, I have finished the course, I have kept the faith" (2 Tim. 4:5-7, NASB).

There will be disappointment for every leader. Roadblocks will appear along the way. The faithful worker must see beyond these obstacles to the Lord who is leading, to the goal that is ahead.

The Sunday School worker loves people.—Nothing takes the place of a caring and concerned leader. Nothing substitutes for a genuine and unfeigned love for people. Concerning the importance and character of love, Paul said, "Faith, hope, love, these three; but the greatest of these is love" (1 Cor. 13:13, NASB). Frances Shaffer wrote a little book, *The Mark of a Disciple*. What was the mark? It was love, of course. Compared to love, everything else is second best. For the Christian leader, love is absolutely imperative. Nothing can or will take its place. Love will succeed when all else fails.

The Sunday School worker seeks and follows the guidance of the Holy Spirit.—The Sunday School worker's effectiveness in the final analysis depends largely upon awareness of and submission to the leadership of the Holy Spirit. The worker knows that attitude, preparation, love, and skills are important; but, also, that he needs the power and influence of the Spirit. Paul said, "I pray that God will help you overflow with hope in him through the Holy Spirit's power within you" (Rom. 15:13, TLB).

SUNDAY SCHOOL LEADERS AND THEIR DUTIES

What leadership positions are needed in a church's Sunday School? What do these leaders do? These questions are answered by grouping Sunday School leaders as follows:

General officers

Officers common to all age divisions

Leaders in the Preschool Division only

Leaders in the Youth Division only

Leaders in the Adult Division only

Leaders in Bus Outreach and Children's Worship

1. General officers

Every Sunday School needs four basic general officers:

   a. Pastor

Let it be clearly understood that the pastor is not a bystander in relation to the Sunday School. As pastor of the church, he is a key leader in the Sunday School. He does not run it or control it. He works with fellow staff members and the Sunday School director to assure that the Sunday School fulfills its purpose.

The pastor should lead the church to have a challenging Bible teaching program with major efforts in Bible study, outreach, witness, ministry, and worship. The pastor is responsible for the following actions:

- Lead the church to have an aggressive program for reaching Christians and non-Christians for Bible study.
- Lead the Sunday School to be positively evangelistic by training Sunday School workers to witness to lost persons in daily contacts and structured visitation and by being alert to evangelistic opportunities in regular Bible study sessions.
- Lead the church to use organizational plans and curriculum resources that best meet the needs of its membership.
- Assist in making available adequate training for all workers; lead in training activities as appropriate.
- Assist the Sunday School director in annual planning.
- Share information about potential workers; lead the church to adopt adequate leadership standards for teachers and officers.

- Participate in and promote Bible teaching projects.
- Lead the church council to involve the Sunday School in stewardship promotion and subscription of the church budget.
- Work with the Sunday School to help workers and members provide caring ministries to members and prospects as needed.

b. Sunday School director

The Sunday School director is responsible to the church for all phases of Sunday School work. He looks to the pastor (and minister of education, if there is one) for counsel and leadership. The director leads the Sunday School and represents the Sunday School on the church council. He is the leader of the Sunday School council.

The Sunday School director's full responsibility includes outreach, Sunday School leader training, teaching improvement, and Bible teaching projects. The director may delegate some of these responsibilities to one or more associates.

c. Secretary

The general secretary is responsible to the director for compiling and maintaining records and reports for the Sunday School.

d. Vacation Bible School director

The Vacation Bible School director is responsible to the Sunday School director for operating an effective Vacation Bible School. The pastor or minister of education often serves as the Vacation Bible School director.

In addition to the four basic general officers, many churches will need one or more of the following officers:

e. Assistant director

The assistant director may be the only general associate, aside from the secretary, in smaller Sunday Schools and is responsible to the Sunday School director for performing assigned duties. The duties usually include one or more of the functions of evangelistic outreach and inreach visitation, leader training, and teaching improvement.

Churches with multiple or satellite Sunday Schools may have an assistant director in charge of each.

f. Outreach director

The outreach director is responsible to the Sunday School director for leading the Sunday School in reaching, witnessing, and ministering. The outreach director also is responsible for looking at training needs in outreach and witnessing and working with appropriate persons to see that needed training is provided.

g. Minister of education

The full-time staff member called minister of education is considered a general officer and is responsible for working with the pastor in leading and training, and in supporting the Sunday School director. In some churches, the minister of education serves as Sunday School director. In most cases, with the exception of final policy decisions, most of the responsibilities listed above for the pastor would be assumed by the minister of education.

h. Director of teaching improvement and training

The director of teaching improvement and training is responsible for improving Bible teaching-learning in Sunday School. He is responsible to the Sunday School director for discovering training needs of present and potential Sunday School workers and for conducting training activities to meet those needs. Alongside the Sunday School director, this person works closely with the Church Training director in scheduling Sunday School training events.

i. Mission Vacation Bible School director

The mission Vacation Bible School director is responsible to the Sunday School director for leading the church to conduct mission Vacation Bible Schools and Backyard Bible Clubs. He finds and recommends locations, selects projects, requests church approval, sets dates and meeting places, gathers materials, enlists workers, provides for training of these workers, conducts and evaluates the projects, and works with the Sunday School leaders to take appropriate follow-up actions.

j. Bus Outreach director

When a church has a bus outreach ministry, the bus outreach

director is responsible to the Sunday School director for reaching persons for Bible study through a bus outreach.

k. Mission Sunday School director

The mission Sunday School director is responsible to the church Sunday School director or church missions committee for the mission Sunday School. The director may need one or more associates.

2. Officers common to all age divisions

The following job titles cover most of the kinds of jobs to be assigned in a Sunday School. Some churches may not enlist all of these workers in all areas of a Sunday School. For instance, in a small Sunday School the department leader or the teacher might assume additional responsibilities.

a. Department director

The department director is responsible to the Sunday School director (or division director) for the work of the department. The director's work includes organizing the department for effective outreach, teaching, and ministry; enlisting and training leaders; administering the department's work; leading department meetings; and leading in planning for Bible study.

b. Secretary

The secretary is responsible to the department director for handling all matters related to department records. In the Preschool Division, this secretary may serve the entire division where there are two or more departments.

c. Teacher

The teacher is responsible to the department director for carrying out the total work of the class or group. The teacher's work includes responsibility for Bible teaching, outreach, witness, ministry, and worship.

d. Department outreach leader

The department outreach leader is responsible to the department director for planning the efforts of the department in outreach, witnessing, and ministry. In the Preschool Division, the department director serves as the outreach leader. In Children's departments, the outreach leader may serve also as a teacher or secretary. When there is no department secretary, the outreach leader maintains the department records.

    e. Division director

The division director is responsible to the Sunday School director for coordinating the work of a specific age division. This position is recommended in all Preschool Divisions when there are two or more departments. Guidelines for determining the need for division directors may be found in age-group books in the "Basic Series."

3. Leaders in the Preschool Division only

    a. Extended session lead teacher

The extended session lead teacher is responsible for planning and directing the teaching-learning experiences that take place during the extended session.

    b. Extended session teacher(s)

The Preschool extended session teacher(s) teaches during the session extended through the worship service, ideally under the leadership of one of the Sunday School or Church Training teachers.

    c. Visitor-teacher

The visitor-teacher in the Cradle Roll department visits in homes of Cradle Roll members.

4. Leaders in the Youth Division only

    a. Class leader

The Youth class leader works with the teacher to correlate and implement all class activities related to learning, outreach, ministry, and outgrowth of Bible study and fellowship. A class needs one or more leaders. The number should be determined by the size of the class, by the ministry needs of class members, by the number of evangelistic and outreach prospects, by the number of fellowship activities, and by the potential leadership abilities of the available youth.

The class leader(s) relates directly to the teacher and works with the department team. Each teacher may either appoint or ask the class to elect the class leader(s), who may serve for a quarter or longer.

5. Leaders in the Adult Division only

a. Department activities leader

The department activities leader works with the outreach leader in weektime activities and has major responsibility for ministry; he also assists in other administration and outreach work as requested.

b. Class outreach leader

The class outreach leader is elected by the church. He works with the teacher and gives direction to the work of reaching prospects and encouraging class member involvement in witnessing to unsaved persons.

c. Group leaders

The group leaders of the class work with the teacher, the outreach leader, and the activities leader in the work of ministering to and reaching members and prospects and encouraging group members in witnessing to the unsaved.

d. Class secretary

The class secretary maintains the records.

e. Class activities leader

The activities leader works with the outreach leader and department activities leader in week-time class activities and carries major responsibility in ministry and fellowship, along with other duties as requested.

f. Homebound visitor

In a Homebound department, the visitor goes regularly to the homes of members assigned for ministry, for sharing Bible materials and engaging in Bible study.

g. Young Adult Away department correspondent

The correspondent has the same relationship to the persons assigned as a teacher has to a class; but he must teach, care, and provide a personal spiritual ministry to group members by letter, by telephone, and through family rather than by face-to-face contact.

6. Leaders in Bus Outreach and Children's Worship

a. Bus captain

A bus captain is elected by the church and is responsible to the bus director in the development of the route (or for the planning, conducting, and evaluating of the work of the route).

b. Bus driver

A bus driver may be elected by the church and is responsible to a bus captain for driving the bus on the assigned route.

c. Assistant

A teenage or an adult assistant may be elected by the church and is responsible to the bus captain for assisting on a route as assigned.

d. Children's worship leader

The Children's worship leader is a church-elected leader who is responsible for the Children's worship service.

e. Children's worship associate

The Children's worship associate is one who assists the Children's worship leader in the Children's worship service. An associate is needed for each group of six to eight children.

THE DISCOVERY OF SUNDAY SCHOOL WORKERS

Being a Sunday School worker, as indicated by the duties, is demanding work. But God has given needed gifts to persons. There are obvious and known needs in the Sunday School for gifted, committed leaders to help the Sunday School do its work. From where do these leaders come? How are they discovered? Where will they be found?

Pray for Leaders

Prayer is the place to begin search for needed workers. We can talk all we want, work with all diligence—and we should do both—but prayer is the essential beginning in a fruitful search for workers. Jesus said to his disciples, "The harvest is plentiful, but the laborers are few; pray therefore the Lord of the harvest to send out laborers into his harvest" (Matt. 9:37, RSV).

Often prayer is the *last* thing we do—not the *first*—in our quest for workers. I often have said: "I have looked and talked and asked, but no one is willing. Where do I go? What do I do?" Then it occurs to me: Have I prayed? Prayer often is the missing ingredient in the search for additional workers.

Sensitize Leaders to Needs

Often some members and leaders are unaware of the workers needed in the church. There are good ways to lead people to be sensitive, aware, and responsive to needs. One way is to ask the pastor to speak to the congregation about the needs. The pastor will know effective ways to lay a biblical foundation and issue a spiritual challenge. I have learned from my close association with four pastors that carefully chosen and well-timed encouragement from a pastor can be used by the Holy Spirit to lead people to respond to worker needs.

Teachers of Adult classes can be asked to observe carefully the gifts of class members and submit names of those that they believe have potential for Sunday School leadership. This is a productive way of discovering leadership possibilities. As a minister of education for twenty-five years, I made a practice of observing, listening, and constantly asking questions, seeking to discover potential Sunday School leaders.

Compile a List of Possible Workers

A list of potential workers should be compiled and maintained. The nominating committee might lead in a churchwide effort to discover workers. The primary source of such a list is, of course, the resident church membership roll. Actually, this is the source for all workers. All other sources simply provide additional information about the persons on the church roll. What are these sources of further information?

Study Sunday School membership.—A search of the Adult Sunday School rolls should make known persons who are actively involved in the Sunday School. Adult teachers are able to recommend persons whom they already have encouraged to accept places of responsibility.

Evaluate Vacation Bible School workers.—Vacation Bible School workers who have not been enlisted as teachers in Sunday School are excellent potential teachers.

Consider Preschool extended session teachers.—Persons enlisted to serve in a Preschool department during the extended session (during worship service) many times receive their first experiences in teaching at church. These persons might have developed special skills that would qualify them as Preschool workers.

Use new member orientation.—Leaders of new church member training classes may be able to recommend qualified workers who have transferred membership into the church. Some new members may be ready to begin serving immediately.

Use leader training course lists.—The director of teaching improvement and training is a valuable resource for prospective workers. Persons who are enrolled in the potential leader course should be considered for service in Sunday School.

Conduct surveys.—Christian service survey cards may be used to discover prospective workers. The cards may be distributed to persons in attendance at church or mailed to the membership.

Gift Search.—This project suggests a person-centered, spiritual approach to turning jobs into ministry. (See *How to Improve Bible Teaching and Learning in Sunday School: Pastor-Director Guide,* pp. 72-73.)

Ask members of the congregation.—A request can be made to the members of the congregation to write names of possible workers on an envelope or card and turn it in to the Sunday School director.

Review drop-out workers.—Leaders who have dropped out or performed poorly in the past may be ready to serve in Sunday School work once again. Some persons who previously felt that they could not serve may now be able to do so.

Now a final word. Since we have said that every Adult member of the church should be considered, the following questions should be asked concerning each member:

Could the person serve if he would? Would this person be acceptable to the church according to the standards of the church? Would this position help the potential worker discover how to use his/her special gifts and thus find fulfillment in serving?

ENLIST WORKERS PERSONALLY

Worker enlistment is the responsibility of the church nominating committee, which should seek to match persons and their gifts with the jobs to be done. Individual gifts, of course, should be considered, as well as the priority needs of the church and its organizations.

It is the nominating committee's job to lead in staffing all church-elected positions filled by volunteers and to keep them filled throughout the year. This committee also should lead in churchwide efforts to discover qualified persons as workers.

Basic Approach

The basic approach of the nominating committee in relation to the enlistment of Sunday School workers is as follows:

The committee selects and presents to the church for election the Sunday School director. Following his election, the director meets with the nominating committee, which serves as a clearing house for all potential workers to be enlisted. The Sunday School director decides on division directors or Sunday School department directors and clears their names with the nominating committee before enlistment. In a small Sunday School, he enlists teachers in the same way.

The division or department directors submit names of teachers and other workers desired to the director and the nominating committee for approval. Then the division or department directors enlist the teachers and other workers. In an Adult department, the department director involves the department outreach leader and the respective teachers in the selection of class out-reach leaders.

Adult teachers submit the names of class outreach leaders to their department director, then to the Sunday School director, who in turn clears with nominating committee before teachers enlist outreach leaders.

The outreach leaders, in cooperation with the teachers and department outreach leaders, then lead in organizing the classes and securing class officers.

Proper Perspective

Worker enlistment time is a time for reevaluation; a time for beginning again. It is a time for changes, a time for new persons in new places. It is an exciting time, fraught with consequences of eternal significance. It is a time to be welcomed as an unparal-leled opportunity to improve the work of the Sunday School. If there are enough workers enlisted and they are enlisted in the proper way, the morale of the Sunday School can improve greatly.

Using annual enlistment time as a "get-rid-of" time for all persons not serving effectively should *never* be our approach. We should always seek to be redemptive, not destructive. We should ask the questions: Is this person serving in the right place? Does this position utilize the individual's true gifts? Is there any other place of leadership that would fit the person's gifts better? If so, how can we lead him to *want* to change to another position? Or perhaps he is in the position that suits his gifts but is not perform-ing effectively. Then, the question becomes: How can we lead this person to a point of effective performance?

Principles for Enlistment Practice

I believe that there are some principles of enlistment that apply to workers for all age groups in the Sunday School. Enlistment will be more effective if these principles are observed.

Enlist each person face to face.—Enlistment should not be

done in a group. It should not occur in a casual hallway conference. It is best not done on the telephone. It is effectively done in one's office or home. Wherever the conference takes place, it should be personal.

Explain all that is required and expected.—It is inexcusable to enlist persons by saying: "There isn't much to do and it won't be very hard." Why have the job then? If one is not told what to do at enlistment time, he cannot be expected to do what he was not asked to do and did not agree to do. Sharing what is required means also stressing the importance of the job. I once made an appointment with a busy executive to offer him a job in Sunday School. I started telling him the duties of the job when he suddenly stopped me and said, "Harry, I want to know one thing about the job before you give me the details." I said, "What is it?" He answered, "I want to know *how important* the job is. I already have enough jobs. Is this job as important or more important than those I have?" I got the point. Since that day, I always have tried to communicate the real importance of the job to a potential worker.

Ask for thought and prayer.—We seek to enlist persons for spiritual leadership. It is logical and right that we should ask the one being enlisted to make the request a matter of careful thought and prayerful consideration. Do not ask for a yes or no unless prayer has been offered. Ask the potential worker to ask God's guidance and make plans to talk again later. Assure the person that you also will be praying.

Let the Sunday School worker be enlisted by the person to whom he will be responsible.—It is a wise practice for the potential worker to be contacted by the person to whom he will be responsible. This plan paves the way for better communication and understanding later. The enlister tends also to feel a responsibility for the one he enlisted. Likewise, the enlisted person appears to feel a sense of responsibility to the one who enlisted him.

By way of commitment, the potential worker should be asked four questions: (1) Will you be regular in attendance? (2) Will you attend weekly workers' meetings and make good preparation to teach? (3) Will you participate in the training provided for you? (4) Will you be involved in outreach and witness? These questions come from the heart of the task of the Sunday School. They involve reaching, teaching, and witnessing.

What about a worker's doctrine and Christian life-style? Questions of this nature should be explored early in the process. The above questions should not be asked until the other facts are known.

Be rigid in principle but flexible in application.—Is every potential worker eliminated when he cannot affirmatively answer all these questions? No. One principle of enlistment that I have learned through the years is to be rigid in principle but flexible in application. This means simply that the principle will not be changed (attendance, training, weekly workers' meetings, outreach, and witness), but some exceptions will be recognized. That recognition is a fact of life but it does not change the principle. Let the exceptions be minimal and continually hold up the principle.

Worker enlistment time can be a happy, exciting, and productive time. Adequate workers *are* in our churches. Let us seek them out and pray them out. The Lord will provide workers for his church.

DEVELOP WORKERS THROUGH PROPER MOTIVATION

"Our workers know what to do; they just don't do it." "The biggest frustration I have is getting people to do what they already know to do." Have you ever heard these statements, or similar? The answer lies in motivation.

Every pastor and every staff member is constantly faced with the question: "How can I lead my people to want to do the job and then do it?" Every Sunday School director, every department worker, and every teacher asks: "How can I lead my department and class members to visit and to witness?" "How can I lead them to participate in training, caring, and ministering?" These are

practical and important questions. They deserve good answers, and there are good answers.

First, a word of caution. Do not confuse motivation with manipulation. A manipulator uses other people as things or objects. A motivator provides for others a desire or motive (which becomes his own) for actions. The manipulator often is insensitive to others and sometimes uses deception and guilt as vehicles. The Christian motivator has respect for the dignity and integrity of the person. He cares about the person and the work.

How is motivation triggered within an individual? What is its source? What are some ways to develop motivation within persons? Here are some ideas I have found helpful:

Example.—People are motivated by the example of others. A life-style that is consistently lived out before others is important; it is a strong factor in motivation. For instance, my own deep love for God's Word can be traced not only to godly parents and Sunday School teachers, but to the example of J. W. MacGorman, professor of New Testament at Southwestern Seminary. Dr. MacGorman was assistant pastor in my home church in Austin, Texas, when I was a teenager. His devotion and commitment to a serious study of God's Word was motivational in my love for Scripture. Mrs. G. M. Smith, longtime Adult Sunday School department director at the University Baptist Church in Fort Worth, provided an example of commitment to visitation and weekly workers' meetings that was a source of inspiration to me and to all of her fellow workers. We were motivated by the example she set before us.

Competence.—Not only do people admire and respect competence and skill in leaders, but their own motivation is triggered by it. It is common knowledge that Tom Landry, for years coach of the Dallas Cowboys, has one of the most astute minds in the game of football. He not only is brilliant, but he is prepared. His players have said about their coach: "You follow Tom Landry because you *know* he *knows*. You know he has done his homework. You have confidence in him." Sunday School teacher, department director, pastor, minister of education—all must know their work. Their people must *know* that they *know*.

Enthusiasm.—Practically everyone agrees that enthusiasm leads to motivation. Enthusiasm is contagious. There are countless illustrations all around us. John Bisagno, pastor of the First Baptist Church, Houston, is the most positive, enthusiastic person I have ever known. I became enthusiastic about things that excited him. First Baptist members caught his enthusiasm. It swept the church. Enthusiastic leadership in the Sunday School will open doors to achievement. Enthusiasm is a spiritual attitude and it communicates to the human spirit.

Commendation.—All of us appreciate a word of commendation and praise. Is there any among us that does not like to hear: "You did such a fine job. Thank you for your splendid work." There are so many opportunities in Sunday School work to express appreciation. How important it is to write a letter or make a telephone call expressing appreciation or offering encouragement. Why don't we do it more often?

A word of caution is appropriate. Never, never praise when you do not mean it. That is flattery. It is deceit. It is not Christian. Praise and commend only when it is earned. Praise privately and publicly.

Consistency.—People are motivated by consistency. They like to feel they can count on their leader to be consistent. Consistency instills confidence and follow-ship. It suggests stability and permanance. Buryl Wilson was director of a twelfth grade department for years at University Baptist, Fort Worth. When Sunday morning came, Buryl was there, prepared. At weekly workers' meeting time, he was there. At weekly visitation, Buryl was there. His workers were inspired and challenged by his consistency. Much of the disappointment experienced in Sunday School work is, at its root, caused by inconsistency on the part of leaders.

Teamwork.—Teamwork produces motivation. When the team begins to pull together, to act as one, to think as one, the work goes forward. Can you imagine a pass receiver for the Pittsburgh Steelers saying: "Hey, I'm going to run my pass pattern exactly as I please. Just get the ball to me." By the same token, can you imagine a Sunday School teacher saying: "I'm going to teach whatever topic I wish to. I'll come to workers' meetings if I have time, and I'll visit if I feel like it." Teamwork is as crucial to the functioning, achieving Sunday School as breath is to life.

Goal setting.—Whether we admit it or not, most of us are motivated by goals. We do not like to be trapped by goals nor considered a failure if we do not achieve them. We do like and respond to reachable and challenging goals. To illustrate, the Leader Training Department at First Baptist Church, Houston, was highly successful. I believe that a part of the reason lay in the fact that clear, realistic, yet challenging goals were set. Each person knew he had to read, study, and report on certain books, attend a definite number of sessions, and participate in practice teaching. Requirements and goals were clear. The students understood, responded, and achieved.

Follow-up.—Follow-up is often thought of as "snooper-vision." It is far more. It is inspection with a view to moving toward goals and objectives. Often we are good in assigning, but weak in follow-up. For instance, we assign prospects to be visited, but do not check to see that the visits were made. We take a census and discover prospects; we even prepare visitation cards. Then we fail to assign the persons' names for visitation. The question about all our plans is: Does anyone follow up to see whether the objective is reached? It is said that Vince Lombardi, former coach of the Green Bay Packers, evaluated *every* player on *every* play of *every* game. That is follow-up.

Love.—Love is the greatest motivating factor of all. Love succeeds where all else fails. Simple, honest, sincere love cuts through when nothing else makes a dent. Love says: "I believe the best about you." Love reaches out and says: "You are important. I really care about you. I believe in you."

Earl Mead, for thirty-seven years minister of education at the

Cliff Temple Baptist Church in Dallas, Texas, contributed to my life in innumerable ways. Dr. Mead said to me when I was a young minister of education: "Harry, love your people. Love all of them. Play no favorites; each is important. Keep each person in your circle of love. Never cast one out. Never criticize your people. Love them." That advice has stayed with me. Why is love the greatest motivator of all? Simple. Look at the source of love. Where do we learn to love? Look to the *cross!* God loved. Jesus loved. He cared. He gave all. We are to be like him. And it is when we love that we are most like him.

PREPARE WORKERS FOR WORK

Sunday School workers are ill-prepared to do their work without proper and adequate training. There is no shortcut for effectively equipping the workers. It has been said that "the difference in churches is leaders and the difference in leaders is training." Leaders are, indeed, the stackpole around which everything takes place. It is a tragedy of inestimable proportion to allow untrained leaders to serve in our churches. We may have to enlist untrained workers, but we do not have to leave them untrained. We will not solve the problem in a short time, but we can take giant strides in solving the problem when we give training the priority it must

Exploring Training Opportunities

There are a variety of training events and activities, some of which are appropriate for churches of every size and shape. What are some of these varieties of training?

Church Study Course.—The Church Study Course provides the basic means of training workers. It contains leadership training books for Sunday School workers in administration, Bible study, doctrine, and other subject areas, and in all the age groups. They are well written and contain much valuable information and help. They are, in fact, a huge storehouse of valuable resources. These books may be read and studied with great profit either in a class or by individual study. All have teaching suggestions and many have resource kits for the persons who lead the group studies.

An encouragement and, certainly, a motivational force is the use of the Sunday School Leadership Diplomas to train workers. Six diplomas are available, each of which calls for six basic books: General officers, Adult, Youth, Children, Preschool, and Special Ministry. In addition, the Sunday School Advanced Leadership Diploma may be earned by workers who have completed the basic diploma and qualified for course credit on eight specific books in eight different study areas.

A third diploma is the Bible Survey Diploma, awarded to persons who complete the six required books in the Bible Survey Series.

The annual edition of the Church Study Course Catalog contains information on the various diplomas, as well as how to request awards and diplomas and how the Sunday School and other organizations can use the system to promote more training in the churches.

Church Training.—I wish to go on record: Church Training has contributed enormously to my own personal growth and development. I am a better person and worker because of Church Training. The churches I served depended upon Church Training for much of the leadership training as well as member training.

Church Training with its ongoing curriculum and equipping center approach offers many excellent training opportunities for our churches to train leaders.

Training potential workers.—Workers can and will accept training before beginning their responsibilities. The Convention Press book *Training Potential Sunday School Workers* offers a workable plan for training leaders. It is specifically designed for potential leaders, but it may be used for training present workers as well. This training can be offered on such a schedule as to permit both on-the-job training and training for potential workers.

Another Convention Press book, *Training Outreach Workers*

for the Sunday School, is particularly suited for offering training to workers with outreach responsibilities.

On-the-job training.—A potential worker may participate in on-the-job training. In short, this involves enlisting a worker, providing textbook and material for study, and arranging for observation of effective Sunday School leaders' performing their tasks. Following and during study and observation, opportunities to practice teach may be provided.

Sometimes it is necessary to enlist a worker who is not adequately trained. At all times there are some people who begin teaching before they are adequately trained. These people need on-the-job training. Conferences with experienced workers or staff members, reading and cassette listening programs, and individual study can be proposed for such people. Frequent evaluative discussions by those who work with inexperienced workers will be helpful.

Convention, state, and association training events.— Ridgecrest and Glorieta are training opportunities of unparalleled value. When a church sends some of its workers to these mountaintop conference center events, revolutionary changes and improvements often occur. Many churches budget for this type of training and provide a portion of each worker's expense to these summer assembly training centers.

State and associational events also offer increasingly helpful training. Various states and associations offer "Glorieta West" or "Ridgecrest East" conferences. They are quality training events. Associations are the "backbone" of training for many churches. They offer various helpful training opportunities for churches of all sizes. The annual associational training school is an example of the excellent training offered by associations.

Individual study.—The individual study plan in the Church Study Course allows a person to study the course materials at his own convenience and speed. When the book is read and the "Personal Learning Activities" are completed, the worker receives credit for the book. Many of the Church Training equipping centers also offer plans for individual at-home study.

Weekly workers' meetings.—While specifically designed for planning the reaching and teaching tasks of the Sunday School, the weekly workers' meeting is, in fact, a splendid training ground for present and potential workers.

Developing a Training Plan for Workers

Having surveyed various training possibilities, let us now look at suggested steps to take for developing and implementing an effective training program.

Create a climate for training and equipping.—Talk about the need, publicize it in the weekly church newsletter or Sunday bulletin, in the pulpit, and in department announcements. It is imperative to get the message out. Some churches adopt a policy on training and make this policy known when workers are enlisted.

Provide financial resources in the budget.—Some training events will require expenditures. A church wisely provides the needed training expenses in the budget. It is an investment in the present and the future, which is returned manyfold.

Prepare a calendar of training.—Take a look at basic training needs. Decide what is needed. Determine when the training can be offered and then provide a calendar of training. When people know what is coming and when, they will more readily participate. Such an approach also assures that you can offer a balanced training plan.

Recognize leaders who train.—Sunday School workers generally do not participate in training for recognition alone; yet, they should be recognized in some acceptable form. Names of those participating in training events may be published. Sunday School Leadership Diplomas should be presented in a formal and affirming way. Letters of appreciation and public expressions are certainly in order. These actions say to the workers that the church values their service and their search for excellence in their work.

Encourage workers to train continually.—Training should occur fifty-two weeks of the year. The need for training leadership never ends; therefore, the need for training never ends. Offer training opportunities every week. Ask and expect workers and potential workers to participate. They will respond in ever-increasing numbers. We must never let up on this ever-present need. We must go on training as we realize "not from the clouds, but from the crowds" come our workers.

Chapter 5

The Sunday School Is . . . Planning Ahead for Effective Work

"Be sure that everything is done properly and in a good and orderly way" (1 Cor. 14:40, TLB).

Paul's advice to the church at Corinth applies to our churches and Sunday Schools in the 80s: "Be sure that everything is done properly in a good and orderly way" (1 Cor. 14:40, TLB). Good planning does not insure results, but it makes them far more possible. Good planning is not the end; it is a means to the end. Good planning is not sacred, but it is essential.

WHAT IS TO BE PLANNED?
Mission Determines Direction

What is there to plan in the church? Why bother to go to those seemingly unnecessary and wasteful meetings? The answer to these why-bother questions is obvious: You will know what to plan and what is necessary when you know what your mission is. Mission determines direction.

Direction is of great importance to people. A person who has no direction often lacks drive and motivation, and appears as a ship without a rudder. Churches that do not have direction and purpose tend to flounder. A sense of direction is nearly always a key factor in progress.

A Sunday School may get a sense of its own direction by looking straight into the mission of the church. The question to be asked is, Does what we are doing in Sunday School actually support the mission of the church? All Sunday School plans must be measured in terms of their support of the church's mission.

Whereas the church's mission is to "make disciples" and "teach them to observe," the Sunday School's task in this mission is to enroll people in Bible study, seek to lead them to Christ, and give guidance to the saved in learning, witnessing, worshiping, and ministering. If that work is to be done, plans must be made. The mission will not be accomplished by slipshod and half-hearted attention to planning. We must decide how to accomplish the mission. That is what planning is all about.

Goals Reflect Mission

Plans should include goals. Sunday School goals are influenced by church goals. Sunday School goals can be broken down into department and class goals. Class goals are broken into group goals. As an example, a church of 800 members sets the following goals:

100 new church members
60 new persons for baptism
50 Sunday School workers trained to witness
50 Sunday School workers trained to teach the Bible
$400,000 pledged to the budget
400 tithers
1 mission Sunday School
1 mission Vacation Bible School

The Sunday School council will look at church goals and at Sunday School opportunities and determine what should be done to help the church accomplish its mission.

WHO DOES THE PLANNING?

Will planning be left to chance? Who will initiate and organize it? Who will see that planning actually happens?

Church Council

Sunday School planning must, of course, relate to church

planning; and basic church planning is done by the church council. The Sunday School director is a member of the church council and represents the Sunday School in church planning. When the church council has determined goals for a given year, the Sunday School council begins to ask: How can we support these church goals through ongoing Sunday School work and through special emphases? Suppose that one church goal is to baptize one hundred persons in one year. The Sunday School may support that goal by emphasizing Bible study enrollment, weekly evangelistic visitation, and witness training. The work that the church council does is an important part of Sunday School planning.

Sunday School General Officers

The Sunday School general officers are central in Sunday School planning. The pastor, minister of education (if there is one), Sunday School director, associate director, outreach director, general secretary, and other general officers make up this planning team. They will plan for the Sunday School council's involvement in planning the total Sunday School program.

Sunday School Council

The Sunday School council consists of all Sunday School general officers and department directors. In churches not having department directors, Youth and Adult teachers serve on the Sunday School council, along with Preschool and Children's directors. Some churches elect division directors. These persons serve on the Sunday School council in addition to, or in place of, the department directors. This council is an absolute must for effective Sunday School work. It is the group that does goal setting and detailed planning—short-term and long-range—for the Sunday School.

Age-Group Divisions and Departments

Planning must penetrate the division and department level.

Some plans move from the church council to Sunday School council to division and/or department level. Department leaders bring to their workers the goals and implementation ideas from the Sunday School council. Workers then discuss goals and try to determine how the department can be supportive of and involved in the plans made for the total Sunday School.

WHEN IS PLANNING TO BE DONE?

Should planning be left to chance? Not if achievement is desired and expected. Planning precedes success. There must be annual, monthly, and weekly planning.

Annual Sunday School Planning Retreat

The Sunday School council can spend highly productive time in an overnight or all-day retreat. It is good, if possible, to get away from the church building at a retreat facility where concentration of participants can meet the challenges of the new year facing them. It may be that someone's home is more convenient and suitable.

Date and commitment.—The retreat should be held in late spring or midsummer, *after* the Sunday School director and other officers who make up the council have been enlisted. It is imperative that every council member attend. Schedule the retreat well in advance of the date and inform the leaders. Ask them to make a commitment to attend. If it is impossible for any director to attend, ask him to arrange for a substitute. Do not settle for less than 100 percent representation.

Agenda.—What subjects should a retreat cover? Details of retreat discussions will vary with churches, but agendas likely would be similar. *The Bible Teaching Program Plan Book* is the basic tool needed for planning to plan and for planning. Sunday School Standards also are invaluable. If you were to sit down right now and jot down the really important things that should be covered on an agenda, the list might look something like this:

- What are the church goals for this coming year?

- What total Sunday School and department goals should be set?
- What was accomplished last year?
- What is the record for the past ten years?
- What is the potential for our Sunday School's involvement in church mission and goals—as a Sunday School or as a department?
- Are space and equipment adequate? What can be done to improve them?
- What training should be provided for our workers?
- Is our weekly workers' meeting conducted effectively?
- What are the policies and procedures for our Sunday School?
- What is the curriculum plan for the coming year in each age group?
- What are the denominational suggestions of approaches, projects, or emphases that our Sunday School might use to accomplish Sunday School and church goals?

In one growing church, the leaders considered the annual planning retreat an absolute must for the Sunday School council members. They felt such concentrated planning to be necessary to effective work. The educational staff prepared a looseleaf notebook for the director of each department, providing important information on calendar, budget, policies, and related matters. The notebook was a collection of information that Sunday School workers needed to reference during the year.

Monthly Sunday School Council

Ordinarily it is recommended that the Sunday School council meet monthly. If a church has a weekly Sunday School council meeting (sometimes called weekly Sunday School directors' meeting), it may be acceptable to meet for planning on a quarterly basis. The weekly meetings are excellent for keeping the work moving smoothly, but some evaluation and planning cannot be completed in the short time available each week.

The council meetings may be held at the church or at someone's home. The agenda can be covered under three points:

Evaluate past records and projects.—Look at past records, noting average attendance and highest attendance, and try to identify those members who have become irregular or have dropped out altogether. Look at new members; look at progress on goals set. Consider the good and weak points of work already completed.

Check progress on projects under way.—The council should evaluate the ongoing work. Are the members involved? What is the attitude of members? Do the workers have a clear sense of direction? Are faith, vision, and excitement present and visible?

Plan upcoming projects and programs.—A large segment of time at council meetings will be spent in planning for future ongoing work and special projects, receiving reports, and accepting assignments.

Weekly Workers' Meetings

Weekly workers' meetings offer huge potential to a Sunday School that takes seriously its commitment to mission. The next chapter will deal in detail with weekly workers' meetings.

WHAT ARE THE RESOURCES FOR PLANNING?

When a church takes seriously the commission of our Lord and honestly intends to follow that commission to the best of its ability, then it begins to ask: Where are we going? How will we get there? The answer to the first question implies that a church's purpose and mission must be determined. The answer to the second means that a church must make specific plans to accomplish the goals. Resources are available for that sort of planning.

Plan Book

The Bible Teaching Program Plan Book is produced annually by the Sunday School Board and is a splendid resource for use by church staff and all Sunday School council members. It can be used for annual and monthly planning. Here are some of the contents of the plan book:

- Work sheet for setting Sunday School goals for the year
- Suggestions for developing a Bible teaching program for the year geared to the needs of the particular church
- Special Sunday School program suggestions for the year
- Organization planning chart
- Monthly calendars
- Monthly plan sheets

Church Goals and Calendar

Many churches set annual goals and adopt an annual calendar. The Sunday School planning process should consider carefully all church goals to see what part the Sunday School has in those goals. The Sunday School director should meet with the church council so as to bring Sunday School input to the church council planning sessions. Then what is projected by the church council will become guidelines for the Sunday School council in its planning.

Leadership Magazines

All planning—annual, monthly, and weekly—should reflect careful attention given to *Sunday School Leadership,* a magazine designed for all council members and others concerned with the total Sunday School program. Equally important as planning resources are the age-group leadership magazines (*Adult Leadership, Youth Leadership, Children's Leadership,* and *Preschool Leadership*), especially the summer issues. Each of these has an entire issue devoted to annual planning and each issue is important to ongoing planning in the age groups.

Trends in City or Community

Whether the planning being done is long-range, annual, monthly, or weekly, the persons involved in planning should be alert and aware of the facts about and the trends in the city or community. For instance, will a city or community grow in number or will it decline? In what direction will it grow? What is the profile of the community? Are there developments already planned that will bring new people and vitality to the city?

Facts and trends are readily available. Check first with your associational missions director for any information that already has been gathered. The Chamber of Commerce usually is helpful in providing such information. Public utilities often are helpful in sharing their findings. When the effort is made to discover facts for planning, it usually is rewarding. This approach has great potential for church and Sunday School planning.

Association, State, and SBC Calendar

Church and Sunday School leaders should consult calendars that have been suggested for the association, the state convention, and the Southern Baptist Convention. These calendars will reveal areas of concern and emphasis that should be useful in developing Sunday School plans and calendars.

Sunday School Standards

For planning, no instrument is of greater potential value than the Sunday School Standards. General and age-group Standard leaflets are available free from state Sunday School offices. Sunday School Standards are not new, of course. The Sunday School Standard of Excellence was introduced by Arthur Flake and proved to be of immense value. During most of the 70s decade, Sunday Schools measured their work by the Achievement Guide.

Purpose of the Standards.—The Sunday School Standard provides a measure by which a leader may determine whether a Sunday School is fulfilling its basic purposes. To fulfill those purposes, plans must be made. Use of the Standard will help a church determine its directions for improvement and successful work.

As a young minister of education at Hyde Park Baptist Church in Austin, Texas, I was new, and my knowledge of Sunday School work was limited. At that time, I had no seminary training. I did have great desire and enthusiasm. A wise member of that church directed me to the Standard of Excellence as an instrument for planning and evaluating Sunday School work. I read it and found it to be exactly what my Sunday School needed. The Standard was used with great profit. It is my prayer that today's Sunday School Standards will provide the same kind of help for 35,000 plus Sunday Schools.

Contents of the Standards.—Each Standard provides a checklist, which says to Sunday School planners, "These are the things that we need to be working on if we are to be reaching and teaching all persons within reach of our church." Three areas relate to purpose and five relate to the "how" of achieving that purpose. Note the areas of work to which the Standard speaks:

1. Outreach and growth
2. Bible study
3. Evangelism
4. Member involvement
5. Organization
6. Learning environment
7. Planning
8. Leadership development

The Sunday School Standard calls attention to the minimum requirements in each of these areas for an effective Sunday School.

Use of the Standards.—Let's consider some specific ways in which the Standards can be used by the Sunday School, by departments, and by classes.

They can be used as an aid in planning the year of specific Sunday School work, as they refer to such basic elements as weekly workers' meetings, January Bible Study, Vacation Bible School, visitation and outreach efforts, enlargement, Promotion Day, enrollment goals, leadership and witness training, and budget needs.

They can be used as a guide in implementing work that will meet basic ongoing needs of a dynamic Sunday School. These basic needs include space provision, furniture and equipment, daily worship, fellowship and ministry, worker enlistment, and training.

They can be used as an evaluation instrument. When the Sunday School council meets, it should give careful attention to progress and actions recommended by the Standard. When department workers meet in weekly workers' meetings, they should do likewise. They should make plans and evaluate work based on department requirements given in the age-division Standards. When classes meet, they should carefully evaluate the work of a Sunday School class, using as a guide the requirements of the age-division Standards relating to classes.

Is recognition for meeting requirements of the Sunday School Standard the ultimate objective? Absolutely not! Churches, Sunday School councils, departments, and classes that see the Standard as an end in itself are shortchanging themselves. It is best seen as a planning and evaluative guide, by which Sunday School workers lead persons to more effective reaching, teaching, witnessing, and ministering. It can serve as a uniform plan that will keep a Sunday School on target. Some churches will go far beyond what is called for in the Standard. Others will find in it a continuing challenge. It is hoped that the Sunday School Standards will keep all of us who work in Sunday School on a directional track. When we go beyond Standard requirements, praise the Lord! If we fall below them, let us keep moving forward in improvement.

Through careful planning, Spirit-directed actions, and honest evaluation and improvement, we shall see goals realized and missions achieved in the kingdom of God through the churches.

HOW ARE PLANS COMMUNICATED AND AFFIRMED?

When goals and objectives have been set and are clear and understandable, and when plans to achieve those goals have been carefully and prayerfully made, what remains? Doing the work, following the plans, you say? Well, yes, that's true, but first those plans must be communicated and affirmed. Where and how does this communication take place?

Communication can be made through the weekly church newsletter or the Sunday School workers' midweek bulletin. Or it may be through a personal letter mailed to all Sunday School workers or members. An exciting way to communicate to the Sunday School workers is through a state-of-the-Sunday-School meeting. This is a special meeting of the Sunday School workers to review and evaluate the work of the Sunday School and to communicate plans for the future. Of course, communication effectively occurs through the Sunday School council and weekly workers' meeting.

Communication can be made directly to the church by a weekly church paper (if there is one), through a special called meeting of the church, or through regular monthly business meetings. These reports to the church can be informative and interesting if facts are gathered and thought is given to the method of presentation.

Preparation Week (usually held before Promotion Day) is one of the best opportunities for communicating plans and goals and securing commitment to them. I have a deep conviction that Preparation Week can bring a sense of joy, anticipation, and challenge for a new year. It can instill a sense of spirit and teamwork in Sunday School workers. When all of the workers are brought together for a time of inspiration, information, and direction, Sunday School work can be launched on a note that will set the tone and pattern of work for all the year to come.

Part III

FOCUS ON
IMPLEMENTATION

Chapter 6

The Sunday School Is . . . Conducting an Effective Weekly Workers' Meeting

"Study to shew thyself approved unto God, a workman that needeth not to be ashamed, rightly dividing the word of truth" *(2 Tim. 2:15).*

The work is organized; the workers are discovered, enlisted, and trained; planning is in process; goals have been set. Now what? The officers and teachers of the Sunday School—all of them—must meet weekly to plan for reaching, teaching, ministry, and effective promotion of the work of the Sunday School. The Sunday School meets weekly, and it is logical that the workers meet weekly. There is no shortcut; there is no easy way. Weekly outreach and witnessing and weekly Bible teaching-learning demand weekly planning and promotion.

WEEKLY WORKERS' MEETING—THE GREAT PROBLEM SOLVER

Some people sincerely question the need for a *weekly* workers' meeting. They honestly doubt its value. Or they simply do not want to pay the price. Others honestly view the weekly workers' meeting as a great problem solver. They view it as a long stride toward achieving effective Bible teaching and reaching. They really believe that a good weekly workers' meeting is the best friend they have. They, as I, have experienced its worth.

It is for me a deeply held conviction that the weekly workers' meeting is one of the best ways to solve the twin challenge of reaching and teaching a nation and a world. That conviction has deepened with twenty-five years as a minister of education in both large and small churches. These experiences have convinced me that an effective weekly workers' meeting can be experienced by every church regardless of size. James Smart is correct when he says: "The patient training of teachers is one of the most consistently fruitful and rewarding expenditures of a pastor's time and could be a major factor in the church's rediscovery of the Bible."[1]

The fact is, we must not be satisfied with the present quality of our Bible teaching and reaching. We must not settle for 40 percent Bible study attendance. We must not be content to watch people join the church by letter only. We can and must improve the quality of our Bible teaching and reaching. We can take a giant stride forward by conducting effective weekly workers' meetings.

After discussing what the weekly workers' meeting means to general officers, Gaines Dobbins pictured its meaning to teachers this way: Without weekly workers' meeting, he said, "teachers will be in the worst plight of all—no one will know what the other is planning to do. There is no way to concentrate on common objectives. Problems of common concern cannot be dealt with. There is no stimulus of mind meeting mind in the study of the Bible. All too often, personal preparation is inadequate; purposes and results of teaching are not compared; and what is learned has very little chance of being given expression."[2]

Mrs. G. M. Smith was the director of a Young Adult department for more than thirty years in University Baptist Church, Fort Worth. Through all those years, she held a successful weekly workers' meeting. How did she do it? She had a positive, it-can-be-done attitude. She asked every worker in advance, "Will you attend?" She had a commitment to it, and she led her workers to that same commitment. In building her workers' meeting, she assured herself a forum in which to tackle and solve problems and meet challenges.

WHAT ARE THE ESSENTIAL INGREDIENTS OF A WEEKLY WORKERS' MEETING?

Is there a proper mix for an effective weekly workers' meeting? If so, what are the ingredients? Are they identifiable? Consider the following.

Prayer

Workers need to pray together. They need to pray about one another's needs and about people's needs. When Sunday School workers pray together about the members' needs, when they pray about their own needs, they develop a caring and loving fellowship. God's presence is recognized. He is near and answers. A weekly workers' meeting provides a place and a time for workers to pray together.

Fellowship

Workers need time to spend in fellowship and communication with one another. The truth is, teachers and leaders learn from one another. Locke Bowman has rightly observed: "When we talk frankly with gifted teachers of long experience, we discover quite readily that they have learned best from observing other competent teachers. Nothing is remembered more vividly or is more influential toward changing a teacher's way of working than the simple experience of seeing how a good teacher operates in a normal church setting."[3] This truth leads naturally to another: "If teachers learn primarily from other, more experienced teachers, then the task before the decision makers in church education is to arrange for more opportunities to get teachers together in normal settings where ideas can rub off from one to another."[4]

"If there were no other reason for the weekly workers' meeting, its supply of the need for fellowship would justify it."[5]

Team Spirit

The church whose Sunday School has a good weekly workers'

meeting will have team spirit. Workers will experience a sense of unity and oneness. That is essential to a New Testament church. It is imperative for a Sunday School. Workers from age group to age group need to grapple with common problems and to be aware of and sympathetic with unique problems. Within the department, workers need to talk and plan themselves together on common goals; and they need to be sensitive to the feelings, hurts, and joys of one another.

A Sunday School's workers need to see themselves as a team. A functioning weekly workers' meeting helps make teamwork a fact.

Commitment

If there is to be an effective weekly workers' meeting, there must be commitment on the part of everyone concerned. Workers who regularly attend the weekly workers' meeting tend to bring a serious commitment to Bible study and outreach. They see others in attendance. They see preparation, prayer, and planning. From this group relationship, a more serious commitment to their own task often follows. They become better students. They become more concerned and responsible in outreach. They are open to the leading of the Holy Spirit. They see the needs of others and they respond to them. Commitment becomes contagious.

Correlation

A functioning, effective weekly workers' meeting will certainly involve correlating the work of the Sunday School class with the department and the department with the church. It will assist in reducing conflicts related to the calendar and curriculum. When pastor, Sunday School director, minister of education, and others realize that they are a part of the whole, correlation and coordination of the entire work begins to be realized.

Promotion

Good promotion is a contributing factor in an alive, growing church. A weekly workers' meeting is invaluable in supporting and promoting stewardship emphasis, revivals, visitation, and a multitude of projects that inevitably are channeled through the Sunday School. It is the largest organization in a church and is called on most often to perform major tasks of the church. Therefore, there is no better vehicle for promotion than the Sunday School weekly workers' meeting.

Planning

A good weekly workers' meeting assures that a department will have consistent and effective planning, not only in Bible study but in outreach and ministry events. Many of our failures come from poor, haphazard planning—or no planning at all. This situation must be changed. When there is no coming together for planning, we tend to rely on announcements from the pulpit, letters to workers, word of mouth communication, or numerous phone calls. These are helpful but inadequate. The weekly workers' meeting provides the opportunity for the proposal, discussion, and implementation of plans. Most people respond better to plans that they have had a part in working out. (See age-group books in the "Basic Series" for more help on the function of lesson planning.)

WHAT ARE THE RESULTS
OF AN EFFECTIVE WEEKLY WORKERS' MEETING?

We have discussed the ingredients of a weekly workers' meeting. When these ingredients are present and a good workers' meeting is being conducted, tangible results are inevitable.

Better Bible Teaching-Learning

Solid weekly workers' meetings will produce better teachers. Good teachers and well-planned teaching-learning sessions produce better Bible study experiences. It is that simple. That fact and that alone should motivate us to engage every means to insure a functioning weekly workers' meeting.

Teachers and leaders are crucial to the Sunday School experience. Gaines Dobbins said that the stimulus of a new building, a sense of duty, and devotion can sustain a Sunday School where teaching is at low ebb, but shoddiness at the heart of the work will someday most surely result in failure.

In my early years as a minister of education, my pastor and I became concerned about multiple activities in a church. We were concerned about taking people away from their families. We should have been concerned, but our response proved to be unwise. We led our people to go from a weekly workers' meeting to a monthly workers' conference. In dismay, we watched the results. Teacher preparation was minimal. Communication was weak. One month was too long to wait for personal communication, and letters and phone calls did not compare with face-to-face exchange. Later we returned to the weekly workers' meeting and to more satisfying results. Since that time I have been totally committed to a weekly workers' meeting.

More Effective Reaching

A good weekly workers' meeting bears fruit. Awareness of absentees and prospects is heightened. Teachers and leaders not only are motivated but they make specific plans to reach more people for Bible study, for Christ, and for his church. Planning at workers' meeting is a vital ingredient in the process of outreach. Churches that have well-planned and well-attended weekly workers' meetings usually are successful in reaching people. When time is spent in assigning, planning, praying, and reporting, reaching people usually is the result.

In summary, everyone gains from a sound weekly workers' meeting. The pastor gains. His influence broadens. He has additional competent helpers. His ministry is extended. He has a team of workers at his side. The teachers and leaders gain. They become better teachers and leaders. They have a sense of achievement. The members gain. They become better learners, attenders, and better students of the Word. The Sunday School director gains. He becomes, in fact, a supervisor and coordinator. He has a forum from which to speak and a well-organized and prepared group of workers to lead.

WHAT ARE THE KEYS
TO A SUCCESSFUL WEEKLY WORKERS' MEETING?

All talk of having an effective weekly workers' meeting without paying the price is idle chatter. It is not going to happen. Here are some keys that have led many churches to have effective weekly workers' meetings.

Commitment of Church Leaders

Of paramount importance, the pastor must believe in and want the meeting. That is a basic requirement. If this desire is absent, there will be no effective meeting. The success or failure of the weekly workers' meeting will hinge, in large part, on his interest. The minister of education (if there is one) must have the same basic commitment. The Sunday School director, likewise, must be committed.

Wanting such a meeting, however, is not enough. These individuals must bring commitment to it. It is one thing to believe in something with your mind, but it is another thing to bring commitment and determination to it. That is exactly what must happen.

Priority Scheduling

The weekly workers' meeting must be given priority. There must be no other activities during the time scheduled for the Sunday School workers that would claim the time and attention of the workers who should attend. Not only must conflicts in scheduling be avoided, but adequate time must be allowed for the meeting. One hour and fifteen minutes is highly desirable. Thirty minutes will not suffice. Avoid reducing the time. Set aside the necessary time and give it high priority.

Expectation of Attendance

When workers are enlisted, they must be asked and expected to attend workers' meetings. As minister of education at First Baptist Church, Houston, I asked our Sunday School workers to attend the weekly workers' meeting. The pastor and I asked them openly, positively, and without hesitation or apology. Some workers had to drive as much as thirty-five miles to be present, and they did it. If you do not ask and expect Sunday School workers to attend regularly, they are not likely to do so.

Rewarding Results

Something good must happen to the workers who attend. If it does, they will consistently return. If it does not, they will find reasons to be absent. Workers who find their own work more satisfying because they are prepared for it will support a weekly workers' meeting.

HOW DO YOU BEGIN A WEEKLY WORKERS' MEETING?

Let us assume that the pastor, the Sunday School director, and the minister of education want the weekly workers' meeting. They are committed to it. They are willing to give it priority and adequate time. They are willing to prepare and work at the job. Now, specifically, what steps should be taken?

Observe in Other Churches

Church and Sunday School leaders should seek out churches of comparable size that have successful weekly workers' meetings. They should visit with them, study the meetings, and find out what takes place. They should seek to discover how these churches started their weekly workers' meetings, what makes them successful, and what are the keys to their continued success. They should look at schedules and times.

Use Available Resources

Read all of the material available on weekly workers' meetings.

Reference should be made to the following resources for information:

Guidance materials.—The book *How to Improve Bible Teaching and Learning in Sunday School: Pastor-Director Guide* contains a section on "How to Build the Workers' Meeting." Suggestions are given for beginning a regular meeting, for answering objections, for adopting a schedule, and for maintaining the meeting.

Teaching books.—Study the book *Helping Teachers Teach,* especially Tom Allerton's chapter, "The Importance of Workers' Meetings." The primary thrust of this chapter is to show general officers how to use workers' meetings to improve Bible study. The four age-group chapters offer an excellent overview of Sunday School work for each age group. The age-group books in the "Teaching Series" provide additional helps.

Leadership magazines.—*Preschool Leadership, Children's Leadership, Youth Leadership,* and *Adult Leadership,* along with teacher's periodicals, give support or actual procedures for conducting the age-group meetings. (The procedures for Preschool, Children's, and Youth departments are found in the teacher's quarterlies.) *Sunday School Leadership* offers help to directors in conducting general sessions and in supporting age-group meetings.

Basic Series.—The series of which this volume is a part offers in-depth help to age-group directors and other leaders in strengthening weekly workers' meeting.

Quarterly kit.—*Workers' Meeting Resource Kit* is produced each quarter to help in planning, promoting, and conducting a regular workers' meeting. It is of special help to pastors, Sunday School directors, and ministers of education. It may be ordered, along with other literature, on the Church Literature Dated Form each quarter.

Plan with Church Council

The weekly workers' meeting should be planned through the

church council, in order to give coordination, direction, and strength to the plans. A successful weekly workers' meeting depends upon the cooperation and correlation that the church council provides. The church council can make calendar decisions that are necessary to the success of the weekly workers' meeting.

Secure Church Approval

When plans and details have been worked out through the church council, the recommendation for a weekly workers' meeting is ready for church approval. Ask the church to decide to have the weekly workers' meeting. Whatever the size of the church, if the church makes the final decision, there will be additional support. This is not to say that you cannot or must not start a weekly workers' meeting without the vote of the congregation, but there is greater likelihood of success if you have church approval.

Publicize Meeting and Enlist Workers

When the decision is made to initiate a weekly workers' meeting, use all of the means available to publicize that fact. Use the church paper, the Sunday bulletin, churchwide or department newssheet, and personal letters. Announce in departments and ask the pastor to present the plan to the congregation on Wednesday and Sunday.

Although the Sunday School workers should be aware of the decision, because they have been consulted from the beginning, it is essential now to begin a strong, aggressive effort to secure involvement and support of all Sunday School workers.

Begin with the department directors. They are crucial to success. If a department director is unwilling to be a part of the weekly workers' meeting, he will not ask his Sunday School workers to participate. Moreover, if the director does not want the meeting, he will not prepare for it and it will not achieve its purpose. But, if the director is committed to participation and attendance, he will actively seek the attendance of his fellow workers.

Following the time with the department directors, schedule a meeting of all Sunday School workers—whether there are ten or two hundred—and explain to them the purpose, plan, policies, and schedule proposed for the workers' meeting. Conduct an open discussion and respond to questions in a helpful, nondefensive way. Some of the objections voiced may grow out of real problems that need understanding and solution. Make adjustments based on suggestions and ask for group consensus and approval of the plans to begin the regular meetings. Publicize the day and time of the weekly workers' meeting. Most churches have their meetings on Wednesday night. It is best to provide a minimum of one hour and fifteen minutes for the meeting. If a weekly Sunday School council or Sunday School director's meeting is held before the department meetings, one hour and thirty minutes is needed.

Provide Training for Leaders

The next step is to provide training for the department directors in conducting the department planning meetings. Weekly workers' meetings often fail because responsible persons do not know what should be accomplished in the meeting or how to accomplish it. If the directors are trained by one who knows how to do the job, there is far better chance of success. In the training of the department directors, use the resources listed earlier.

If you are beginning a weekly workers' meeting and there is no one available to train the directors, then go to your association or another church, or ask your state office for help. Enlist an experienced person to train your directors. Choose a time most suited to your workers.

Do not begin your department meeting without giving your directors help in conducting their meetings. Be sure that when the training is concluded, every person who is to lead a meeting has every detail of the first meeting planned.

It is my strong conviction that in any church, whatever its size, workers can gather to plan for Bible study and outreach. In the small church with only one or two workers per age group, excellent meetings can be held under the direction of the pastor or Sunday School director.

Provide for Children and Preschoolers

Make provision for the children of the Sunday School workers. Some churches have mission activities during this period. Others have music activities. Some workers will be unable to attend unless adequate preparation is made for their children. Churches often fail at precisely this point. Responsible parents will not attend weekly workers' meeting when their children have no constructive activities. It may not be easy to have such activities, but it is absolutely essential. Furthermore, these activities are needed for the development of the boys and girls.

Believe You Can!

Perhaps the small church with no staff leadership other than a part-time pastor will feel that it cannot begin a weekly workers' meeting. Southern Baptists have more than 35,000 churches. More than 20,000 churches have fewer than 150 persons enrolled in Sunday School. Some churches worship and study in one-room buildings or in buildings with only a few rooms. In many of these churches, the Sunday School is, for the most part, a class organization. Even so, these churches can have strong weekly workers' meetings.

If a Sunday School is resuming its weekly workers' meeting or seeking to give new life to an existing one, most of the above procedures should be followed.

WHAT FORMAT AND SCHEDULE ARE BEST FOR WEEKLY WORKERS' MEETING

Various schedules may be used for the weekly workers' meeting. The one adopted will depend upon the location, size, constituency, and unique needs of each church. Three possible schedules are given below.

While only three plans are shown here, there are any number of ways the weekly workers' meeting may be scheduled. For instance, a fellowship supper might or might not precede the meeting, and prayer meeting might either precede or follow the workers' meeting. Whatever works best for your church is the best schedule to follow!

Plans 2 and 3 call for all outreach leaders to meet together once a month during the teaching-learning segment. Adult class outreach leaders should be included in this monthly meeting. This meeting should be scheduled so as not to interfere with Preschool and Children's departments' unit planning, which usually is held on the Wednesday preceding the first Sunday of the month.

WEEKLY WORKERS' MEETING

PLAN 1
(for small Sunday Schools)

GENERAL PERIOD (all workers together)   20 minutes
- Administering School Concerns
- Planning for . . . Reaching
                        Witnessing
                        Ministering
- Praying Together

TEACHING-LEARNING PLANNING PERIOD   40 minutes
- All workers together for directed planning of age-group units and lessons (about 30 minutes)
- Special age-group preparation time to prepare room or area of building for Sunday's session (about 10 minutes)

PLAN 2

DEPARTMENT DIRECTORS' PERIOD (meeting in   15 minutes
  separate room from the supper)
GENERAL PERIOD (all workers around supper table) 5 minutes
DEPARTMENT PERIOD   55 minutes
- Administering Department Concerns
- Planning for . . . Reaching
                Witnessing
                Ministering
- Planning for Teaching-Learning (30 minutes)
- Praying Together

PLAN 3

GENERAL PERIOD (all workers together)   10 minutes
DEPARTMENT PERIOD   50 minutes
- Administering Department Concerns
- Planning for . . . Reaching
                Witnessing
                Ministering
- Planning for Teaching-Learning (30 minutes)
- Praying Together

What Actually Happens

Now, let us look closely at a sample weekly workers' meeting to discover what actually happens in the parts of the weekly workers' meeting. Let's use Plan 2 for illustrative purposes:

DEPARTMENT DIRECTORS' PERIOD

Some Sunday Schools find it desirable to have a weekly meeting of the department directors. This meeting is the equivalent of the weekly Sunday School council. A few larger Sunday Schools, usually with age-group ministers, find it more advantageous to meet weekly by divisions for this general period.

If a church does not have age-group ministers, lay age-group division directors can perform the same function. The general

Sunday School director may wish to be in a different division meeting from time to time.

What should take place in the fifteen-minute period with the department directors? It is a time of inspiration. It is a time of information and instruction. It is a time for evaluation and planning. Some things are discussed at this time that can be relayed to the department planning meetings. This period might include the following:

- Review of *Sunday School Leadership* magazine, age-group leadership magazines, and other curriculum materials
- Presentation of future events, such as visitation plans, stewardship emphasis, revivals, and family life emphasis weeks (such as Christian Home Week)
- Evaluation of enrollment and attendance
- Evaluation of effectiveness of teaching-learning
- Testimonies of things accomplished
- Instruction in how to conduct or strengthen department meetings
- Prayer for all the work of the Sunday School

Above all, this time together will build team spirit.

Although it is the writer's belief that the weekly meeting is helpful, many churches meet with the Sunday School council or age division only monthly. A monthly meeting would accomplish much of the above and would allow time in larger blocks for long-range planning.

GENERAL PERIOD

The Sunday School director is responsible for this time. He works with the pastor and/or minister of education in planning and leading the period. Helpful resources include *Sunday School Leadership, Workers' Meeting Resource Kit, Bible Teaching Program Plan Book,* and the church calendar.

This period is primarily one of inspiration and information. It should be brief but meaningful. Use visuals and testimonies. If a Sunday School council or age-division meeting precedes the general period, do not rehash everything discussed there. Your workers will ask, "Why did we attend council meeting if we're only going to get it all again here?" Or they will ask, "Why attend general periods?"

Let's note some items that may be presented during the general period: statistical review of progress; a chart comparing the current year and previous year in attendance on Sunday or at workers' meetings; teacher-member interview to indicate improved teaching or involvement of members in learning; testimony by a member on the the subject, "What I Get from My Sunday School Class"; library or media center feature; plans for a coming revival; calendar for the quarter; goals of the church and their attainment; introduction of new Sunday School workers; recognition of outstanding departments or classes; testimonies on subjects such as, "Why I Visit," "Recent Witnessing Experience," or "This Idea Really Worked"; testimony of a recent convert; report on an experience of reclaiming an indifferent member; frequent sharings from the pastor.

Whatever is included in this general period, let it be happy, positive, and enthusiastic. Let it have a reason and purpose, and then get on to what follows without a loss of time. Stay on schedule. Do not go over the allotted time. Emphasize only a few activities that have priority. Try to select focus events that concern all or nearly all workers.

DEPARTMENT PERIOD

Administering department concerns.—Plan for reaching, witnessing, and ministry. This period is critical to an effective weekly workers' meeting. It should be led by the department director. The director may delegate as he chooses, but the period is his responsibility.

What should take place in this period? The following are some suggestions:

• **Department secretary:** Present a brief report from last Sunday and give a review of the records for recent months.

• **Outreach leader:** Distribute prospect cards to each worker and ask for a report on assignments made the previous week. Discuss absentees and ways to reach absentees and prospects. Promote the church's visitation day plans. (If teachers are absent, visitation assignments may be mailed on the following day or distributed on visitation day or the following Sunday.) Responsibility for outreach should be pinpointed and follow-up planned. Also discuss progress on the Sunday School Standard, training plans, and any social or fellowship events planned by the department.

• **Department director:** Discuss the organization of the department and equipment or supplies needed, along with plans for enlargement. Discuss policies in enrolling new members, concern for attendance, plans for evangelism, and goal setting. Obviously, each of these will not be discussed in detail each week.

It is important to remember that administration and promotion must be planned for just as carefully as Bible study.

Planning for teaching-learning.—This period should be a minimum of thirty minutes, and it is the responsibility of the department director. Most of the time should be spent in preparing for the next unit (called "division" in Bible Book materials) of lessons and/or next Sunday's session. There will be differences in how the various age divisions do their planning, but some things are appropriate for all age divisions.

During this period, the workers will see the next Sunday's study materials in context and will, before the meeting is completed, have planned how the session will be conducted. In the context of planning teaching procedures for coming sessions, some of the following topics may be discussed from time to time: needs of the learners, characteristics of the age group, how learning takes place, what methods or learning activities are appropriate for the age group and the Bible material to be studied, how to secure application of Bible truth, how to study the Bible, good resources for Bible study and for teaching, principles of Scripture interpretation, how to secure involvement and cooperation, how to witness in the context of the Bible study sessions, and how to evaluate the results of teaching.

This period should be as carefully planned as the Sunday sessions, if the Sunday sessions and all other work of the department are to be meaningful.

For more information on how to conduct the department sessions, see the "Basic Sunday School Work Series" book for each age group, the leadership magazines and teachers' periodicals, and *How to Conduct Age-Group Workers' Meetings: Response Manual.*

A Plan for Small Sunday Schools

Sunday Schools with an enrollment of less than 150 and those organized primarily on a class basis may find Plan 1 appropriate to their needs. Here are some further suggestions:

GENERAL PERIOD

This session may begin with Scripture reading and prayer, or a time for prayer may be reserved for the last few minutes of the period.

The general period should highlight upcoming events. Specific plans can be made and promoted. This also would be a good time to deal with administrative matters, to discuss resources, and to focus on general Sunday School goals. Nothing should be planned for this period that would not be pertinent to the entire group.

This period gives a great opportunity for reporting on weekly attendance, recognizing classes that have done a good job, and noting any new members that have joined the Sunday School during the past week or month. This also is a good time to assign prospects, making special plans for visitation, and to project goals for outreach in the future.

TEACHING-LEARNING PLANNING PERIOD

This period in the small Sunday School can be conducted in

one room under the direction of the pastor or another qualified member. By using a plan sheet and the age-group materials, each age-group leader—whether working alone or in teams—can be led to make preparation for the unit or session ahead. Toward the end of the period, the leader may ask workers to share some of their plans. These can be discussed as time permits. Some workers may wish to return to their Sunday morning work area to prepare materials, etc. after the time of joint planning.

While variables within age groups make it impossible to suggest one specific agenda, the following ideas may be helpful in leading the teaching-learning planning period:

1. Distribute plan sheets to any workers who do not have them.

2. Discuss the learners' needs.

3. Consider the aim of the next unit of lessons and plan specifically for next Sunday's lesson.

4. Determine teaching objectives.

5. Determine what methods will best help reach the aims.

6. List the resources needed; make assignments.

7. Review the Scripture lesson or Bible materials.

8. Share ideas about making lesson application in real life.

9. Close with prayer.

HOW IS A WEEKLY WORKERS' MEETING MAINTAINED?

It often is true that a church establishes a weekly workers' meeting only to see it sputter and fail or perhaps never get off the ground. Others limp along for years, doing mediocre work. Sometimes weekly workers' meetings are scheduled because it is "the thing to do." The challenge is to begin and continue a weekly workers' meeting that is effective and profitable. Here are some suggestions.

Share Needed Information and Guidance

Workers need up-to-date, accurate information on the work of the departments and the Sunday School. They need to know about events and goals of the church. They appreciate knowing what is happening in various departments. A weekly workers' meeting newssheet can help. Call it "Table Talk," "Sunday School News," "The Observer," "The Link," or some other title. Whatever its title, give information to Sunday School workers about enrollment, attendance, outstanding classes and departments, future events, and so on. *Motivators for Sunday School Workers* is listed on the Church Literature Dated Form. These sheets, one per month and available in lots of 25, are printed on one side with helpful information for workers. The other side is left blank for local news and information.

Provide Adequate Resources

Provide an 8½ x 11 notebook for each director. (Some churches provide one for each teacher, as well.) Include in this notebook such materials as these:

• Guidelines for Sunday School workers, which might include workers' responsibilities, resources available, general policies of the Sunday School, how to obtain supplies, grading policies, and other pertinent information

• A weekly workers' meeting agenda, giving help on conducting weekly workers' meetings

• Calendar for the year

• Curriculum outlines of all age groups (See *Church Services and Materials Catalog* or summer issues of leadership magazines.)

• Visitation procedures and schedule

• Department and class officers' duties, where appropriate

• Teaching plan sheets for appropriate age groups

Many other helpful items for such a notebook are available. Printed materials may be distributed from week to week, with workers being encouraged to place them in their notebooks. It is amazing to observe the pride that a worker takes in such a simple but helpful tool.

Also call attention to *Media* magazine. Each issue contains a section called "Media for . . .," which lists resources by curriculum lines for each age group. The church that has a well-developed media center (library) can offer better help to its Sunday School workers.

Make Constructive Use of Records

Obtain an attendance report from each department at the weekly workers' meeting. For each department, use a simple folder. Type the names of each worker and department on a sheet. Check attendance each week. Use the folder to distribute any printed pieces you wish your workers to have. Workers will look forward to receiving the department folder. It will take only a few seconds to record attendance. The record will enable the Sunday School director to discover strong and weak points immediately.

Give Attention to Strengths and Weaknesses

When a department begins to drop off in attendance, don't delay action. Talk to the director immediately. Find out what the problem is and help the director take steps to correct it. Problems will not go away by ignoring them. They will only get worse.

Look closely at successful department weekly workers' meetings being held. Find out what is being done that is achieving results. Publicize the actions behind such results. Seek to get other leaders to take similar actions. Capitalize on success. Recognize workers who do outstanding jobs. (See pp. 24-35 in *Helping Teachers Teach* for a good strategy on helping strengthen workers' meeting.)

Provide Ongoing Training to Leaders

Train department directors in how to conduct weekly workers' meetings. Some directors have never seen an effective administrative planning session. Some have not seen an effective teaching planning period. Some directors are self-starters and will find answers to questions, but most do not. They need help.

If a successful age-group meeting is being conducted, ask that other departments be allowed to visit that department at the weekly workers' meeting. Let them observe what happens. Be sure that the observers have orientation before observation and time to talk afterward.

Or, ask the Sunday School director or age-group division leader to have individual conferences with the department directors. Give them weekly plan sheets. (See age-group "Teaching Series" of books and Section 4 of *How to Improve Bible Teaching and Learning in Sunday School: Pastor-Director Guide*.) Show them how to use them. Be sure that they understand how to conduct the workers' meeting. A part of the monthly Sunday School council meeting may be spent in working with directors to increase their competency in conducting workers' meetings.

By whatever means you choose, help directors have a sense of confidence about conducting the meetings. This kind of attention to the work will take time, but the results will make it worthwhile.

BUT WILL IT REALLY WORK HERE?

I am not naive enough to think that there will be no objections to the idea of weekly workers' meetings. Indeed, there will be. These objections will occur in small Sunday Schools and in large ones. Let them come. There is an answer to each objection. These exchanges can serve to clarify the purpose of the weekly workers' meeting and the depth of commitment to do it as a workable way to improve Bible study and outreach. Furthermore, we need to remember that the objections often come from good people who want to do God's work in the best way possible. Most of them are reasonable and will listen and respond. Let's look at some of these possible objections.

Our Sunday School Is Too Small

If you have only fifty enrolled in Sunday School, you may have eight to ten workers. That's twice the number needed on a basketball team and about the same as it takes to fill the baseball team. It's nearly as many as it takes for a "starting eleven" of a football team. Can you imagine team members saying, "We don't need to practice"? The ease or difficulty of a weekly meeting is not related to size. Intelligent and committed Christians work in a small Sunday School. The need for preparation is also unrelated to size. Every learner in a Sunday School—large or small— deserves to have good learning experiences, which require planning and preparation.

We Work with Different Age Groups, Use Different Literature, Teach Different Lessons, and Have Different Objectives

Good. The statement in itself emphasizes the crucial need of coming together. All the more important is the coordination and planning of the many projects of the church. All the more important is the need for fellowship and communication. We must not be separate entities; we must be one family, one body; we must have one mind and heart. We can do our work better when we come together to plan, prepare, and pray.

I Don't Have the Time

I can sympathize with that problem. There are many requests and demands on all of us, and they all take time. Thus, it becomes important to ask: How important is this weekly workers' meeting anyway? It does, indeed, become a matter of priorities. The weekly workers' meeting, when rightly conducted, ranks high on the scale of priorities. What is more, it is a timesaver when properly conducted.

We Don't Have the Leaders Who Can Make It Go

That is a good point and, happily, it can be answered. The solution already has been pointed out in the section on how to conduct the meetings—that leaders should be trained. Your leaders are capable, and training will make them competent. And the workers themselves, by their presence, participation, preparation, and involvement, will make the meetings successful. Directors must be helped to see that leading is not a performance; the director simply acts as a leader while workers talk together and plan together. If the leader has done his best to get ready, the workers will help carry the meeting.

I Just Don't Need It

The statement in itself is suspect. Yet, some persons are perfectly sincere in saying this. But some questions should be asked: "Do you mean you don't need the fellowship of your fellow workers?" "Do you not need the sense of unity and oneness that is possible?" "Do you not wish to be a part of the team?" "Is there no one in the department or Sunday School who could contribute anything to you?" Even if, in sincerity, one could answer no to all of these, then there is yet another approach. "What about sharing your knowledge and gifts with your fellow workers? If it is true that you are a good Bible student, knowledgeable in teaching methods and techniques, would you share your knowledge, ideas, and experience in weekly workers' meeting?" We are on firm ground here, for Scripture reminds us that "much is required from those to whom much is given, for their responsibility is greater" (Luke 12:48, TLB).

It's Just Not Worth the Time

Granted, that is the case in some weekly workers' meetings, and it is deplorable; but it need not be so. For this excuse, there is a question: "What would make it more helpful to you? What would make it worthwhile? What would need to take place for it to be worthwhile to you?" Replies to this question can be suggestions for improvement. Help the workers see that the meeting is actually a timesaver. Plan your promotion. Give all the help possible. Countless Sunday School workers do say, "It is worth it!" Why not the workers in your church?

I Really Can't Attend

Some persons *really* can't. They have training classes that meet at night or are out of town on the meeting night. They just can't attend. Each church must make its own policy, of course, but a reasonable approach may be that if a person teaches or has leadership position, he is expected to attend workers' meetings. Keep that as the policy. Don't lose it. Then make exceptions on those rare occasions when there is good reason to do so. Consider the person teaching the class and who you would have as a replacement if one becomes necessary. For twenty-five years, I have maintained the stated policy, but remained flexible in application. In the doing, I have seen strong and virile weekly workers' meetings contribute greatly to the work of the church.

I Have No Way to Get There

That's not a hard one to answer. If we try, we can help a person find transportation. It is worth it to try.

I Just Can't Get There at That Time

This person sometimes is sincere, sometimes not. If not, try to discover the real reason and respond to it. If it is the time, ask, "When could you attend?" It may be that the provision of a meal at church would solve the problem. If so, try to do it. It may be that beginning one hour earlier or later would be better for most people. If so, adjust the schedule. Or in a few cases, a department may need to meet at a different time from the main meeting. This is not desirable, but it is better than no meeting. The main point is, these people can be led to attend.

¹James D. Smart, *The Strange Silence of the Bible in the Church* (Philadelphia: Westminster Press, 1970), p. 170.
²Gaines S. Dobbins, *Building a Better Sunday School Through the Weekly Officers and Teachers' Meeting* (Nashville: Convention Press, 1957), p. 14. Out of print.
³Locke E. Bowman, Jr., *Straight Talk About Teaching in Today's Church* (Philadelphia: Westminster Press, 1976), p. 130.
⁴Ibid., p. 131
⁵Dobbins, *Building a Better Sunday School,* p. 19.

Chapter 7

The Sunday School Is . . . Reaching People

"Assemble the people, the men and the women and children and the alien who is in your town, in order that they may hear and learn and fear the Lord your God, and be careful to observe all the words of this law" (Deut. 31:12, NASB).

Reaching people is a concept originating in the heart of God. It is the purpose that brought Jesus into the world, a heartthrob that characterizes Christianity. It is the mark of a spiritually vital church. It is evidence of commitment to Christ. It is our response to a spiritually needy and hungry world.

REACHING PEOPLE IS BIBLICAL

The Bible is a book of many books by varying authors, written over a period of many centuries. Yet, one unifying theme permeates all of the Bible materials. God's intention to reach out in loving redemption to all people is clearly the common thread of the entire Word. This idea is embodied in Ephesians 3:11, "according to the eternal purpose which he purposed in Christ Jesus our Lord." In other words, "Gentiles should be fellow heirs of the Kingdom, along with the Jews; fellow members of the same body, the church, and fellow partakers of all the promises given to Abraham."[1]

W. D. Carver, longtime Southern Baptist missions professor, saw this idea summarized in Ephesians 3:6, but fully developed in the Bible as a whole. God's unswerving desire and purpose is to save everyone. That is why Christ came, died on the cross, and rose again—that all people might be saved and taught how to be disciples. We have not done all that God intended when we enroll people in Bible study. But this is where we begin in Sunday School. We go reach, so we can go teach.

The Lord Jesus' command (Matt. 28:19-20) to go into all the world was not made once only, for our Lord, "delivered not so much the Great Commission as a series of Great Commissions, each with its distinctive emphasis, but all for a worldwide task!"[2]

In fact, each of the four Gospels has a statement of the commission, although none tells the whole story. A brief look at the instructions our Lord "gave to his disciples leaves no room for doubt concerning the importance he attached to the plan for witnessing to all the peoples of earth."[3]

In his prayer of John 17, Jesus assumed that his disciples would be going. In this high priestly prayer, Jesus made clear his purpose for the disciples: "As Thou didst send me into the world, I also have sent them into the world" (John 17:18, NASB). It is clear also that his disciples are sent in order "that the world may believe that Thou didst send Me" (John 17:21, NASB).

While Matthew 28:19-20 is one of the clearest statements of our Lord's command to make disciples of the people of the earth, there are many other verses that clearly teach the same thing. Read Luke 24:47-48 and Acts 1:8 for other statements from Jesus.

The apostle Paul felt that he had been set apart to preach the gospel especially to the Gentiles. (See Gal. 1:16.) He also understood our Lord's command that the gospel be carried to all the peoples of the world, in essence to all people, all tribes, and to the ends of the earth.

So the role of the disciples to reach out is clear, and the work is inescapable. The Great Commission is not a chance statement, to be shrugged off by "skeptical or uncommitted disciples, either in the first century or in the twentieth."[4]

REACHING PEOPLE IS INCLUSIVE

We have seen from Scripture that we are to reach out into a world of unsaved people with the good news. We must cross geographic, cultural, and racial lines. The gospel is indeed for all persons and all places. No one is excluded. The "whosoever will" in John 3:16 makes that truth absolutely clear. Surely Christ's death on the cross was for each person. That is the good news of the gospel.

One of the best ways to reach out and touch this vast unreached population is to get people involved in Bible study. We can do so by enrolling them in Sunday School, for Bible study is precisely what Sunday School is all about. *One of the first steps in reaching out then is to enroll persons in Bible study.*

Reach In

Reaching in means leading all of the members of the church to study God's Word—seriously and regularly. Even though we believe that every member of the church ought to be enrolled in Sunday School and involved in Bible study, such is not the case. In fact, there are more than thirteen million Southern Baptist church members and only 7.3 million Sunday School members. Since some of the Sunday School members are not members of the church, the real difference between church members and Sunday School members is even greater. Thus, there are more than seven million Southern Baptist church members not enrolled in Sunday School. Of course, some 3.8 million of the unenrolled are nonresident members. That is all the more reason and challenge for identifying these persons and seeking to involve them in Sunday School and Bible study.

Church leaders should know exactly how many church members are not enrolled in Sunday School: What are their names? Where do they live? What are you doing to reach them? Can you do more? Have you given up? Don't. Many of them can be reached. Be alert, aggressive, and active. Seek to enlist every member of your church in Sunday School. Get them involved in Bible study.

Those members of your church who no longer reside in your town are still your responsibility. The fact that they have never transferred their letters to another church is an indication that they may not be involved in Bible study and may not be pursuing an active church relationship. Send their names and new addresses to the Hello Baptists Desk at 127 Ninth Avenue, North, Nashville, Tennessee 37234. Help a church near them reach out and involve them in Bible study and service through the church.

Reach Out to Special People

If we take seriously the commission of our Lord to go to all people, we will attempt to reach everyone, including some special folk. This commission means reaching those who are sometimes overlooked or ignored, those who may be difficult to reach. Our task calls for special preparation and effort. Reaching special people will require new and unique training. It may even mean reaching out to only a few in some cases. As we consider this type of outreach, we will remember that in the sight of our Lord, each person is unique and important, and each person is worth redeeming.

Deaf.—Approximately 500,000 people in the United States have hearing impairment severe enough to require special provision in situations such as Sunday School. In some churches, deaf persons may be the leaders and teachers in departments and classes for deaf persons. Other churches may provide an interpreter in existing departments or classes. Wherever possible, a separate department usually is desirable.

Blind.—Some people have visual impairment severe enough that special curriculum material—braille or tapes—is required. In the United States, about 6.4 million persons have some visual impairment. Around 1.7 million have severe visual impairment, including the 490,000 who are blind—that is, have no usable vision. As a rule, these persons prefer to be included with sighted persons for Bible study. Churches can and should give careful attention to reaching them.

Mentally retarded.—It is estimated that there are more than 6.5 million mentally retarded persons in our nation, or more than 3 percent of the total population. One family in every ten is touched by mental retardation. These people are important to their families and to society, and they are loved by Jesus. They need and want his love and our love. We must find ways to love and minister to this large group of individuals with special needs, and to their families as well. When we provide for retarded persons, we help their families feel welcome and enable them to become involved in Bible study. Additional information on reaching and ministering to mentally retarded persons can be found in the book, *Reaching and Teaching Mentally Retarded Persons,* by Doris D. Monroe.

Physically handicapped.—Some people have physical handicaps (other than deafness or blindness) that require special provision if they are to participate in Bible study. State and federal laws now require that public buildings be constructed with special provision for the physically handicapped. Ramps, special entrances, and locations are important when adequately providing for the handicapped.

Persons who are unable to attend.—There are people who cannot attend Bible study because of ill health. Several approaches may be taken to reach these people. A Homebound department will be effective in reaching and ministering to such persons. Some churches minister to the homebound through the proper age Sunday School class. A more effective ministry usually occurs when a specific department exists and does this work. The book *Working with Homebound Adults in Sunday School* provides additional information on the Homebound ministry.

Also, a church may establish weektime Bible classes, which, in effect, are weekday Sunday Schools for persons who would attend Sunday School regularly if work schedules permitted. These classes may be held on Wednesday or some other weekday. A fellowship Bible class in a home may reach persons who presently do not attend Sunday School on Sunday. Experience tells us that people will respond to these provisions for Bible study. Records show that in 1979 there were 15,000 such study groups in 8,000 churches, with an enrollment of over 125,000.

Cradle Roll.—The Cradle Roll is effective in reaching out to children under age two who are not enrolled in Sunday School. This ministry also includes expectant parents, both members and prospects. This is an area of tremendous outreach potential. Expectant parents are keenly sensitive to the needs of their expected child. Parents of children under age two are vitally concerned about their children. Most parents are serious about their responsibilities. It is extremely important that the church speak to their spiritual responsibilities as parents. Workers in the Cradle Roll department will seek not only to enroll those under two in the department, but also to lead unsaved parents to Christ and church membership. They will seek also to encourage parents in the spiritual guidance of these children. The entire family is the concern of Cradle Roll.

Of course, workers will seek to lead parents to begin bringing their children to Sunday School regularly. When the preschoolers are brought to Sunday School, they are transferred to their appropriate Preschool department. The Cradle Roll department has tremendous potential to reach out and touch the lives of thousands of parents as well as little children and to strengthen the family in the process.

Language or ethnic groups.—This group includes persons who use some language other than English as their primary language or whose command of the English language requires special provisions. Possibilities for reaching out to language and multiethnic groups across this nation are positively staggering. Out of the population of 215,000,000, ethnic groups make up 57,000,000. And they continue to come in ever increasing numbers. The United States has been called a melting pot. But the truth is, the melting pot has not melted much. Groups are clear and defined. Who will reach out to them? How will the job be done? Perhaps our greatest potential for growth and for ministry lies in providing Bible study for the ethnic and language groups in our nation. The enormous potential is a responsibility and a privilege. Some significant facts about America ethnicity are as follows: There are 2900 language/culture congregations among Southern Baptists, 7700 ethnic groups in the United States, 95 American Indian tribes and subtribes, and 380 churches with ministry to internationals.

The Sunday School Board now provides some printed materials in Spanish, including Sunday School quarterlies for Adult members (*El Interprete*) and teachers (*El Interprete: Maestro*); January Bible Study Adult books; and Sunday School guides for general officers and the four age divisions.

REACHING IS WORK

The program and organization of the Sunday School are developed to mobilize all members and workers in the teaching and outreach work of the church. Class and department structure, worker assignments, visitation approaches, prospect records, prospect discovery activity records, workers' meetings, and Promotion Day are used to motivate and facilitate the reaching and winning of people.

To reach means to enlist and involve persons in Bible study. It means enlisting and involving unsaved persons, unchurched Christians, members of a church who are not a part of the Bible teaching program, and children of these groups.

The basic approach through which the Sunday School involves its workers and members in reaching is prospect discovery and the Sunday School visitation and outreach programs. Let us now look at the details of this reaching process.

Organizing, Training, and Planning for Outreach

How a Sunday School is organized directly affects a church's outreach. If a Sunday School fails to organize for outreach, the result is inevitable: There will be no outreach. A Sunday School organized on an age-graded basis, with the appropriate number of units and with persons assigned to outreach, *will* reach people for Bible study. Such an organization makes it possible to assign responsibility for specific persons to specific classes and departments. A good organization also makes it possible to give clear responsibility for outreach to persons enlisted to lead in that work. The following workers have outreach responsibilities:

1. Outreach director of the Sunday School
2. Department directors
3. Department outreach leaders for all age-group departments (In Preschool departments, the director is the outreach leader.)
4. Class outreach leaders in Adult classes
5. Youth leaders in Youth classes
6. Class group leaders in Adult classes
7. Teachers
8. Members

It is equally important to train workers and members for outreach. While it is possible for one to visit without training, it is better to provide training either before or during participation in the visitation activities. This training may be done by providing conferences on how to visit and witness. One of the best ways to teach workers how to visit is to have on-the-job training. This training occurs when an experienced person and an unexperienced person visit together. This visit should be preceded by orientation and followed by discussion of experiences. Outreach training should be carefully planned and scheduled.

Materials useful in such training include these titles: *Reaching People Through the Sunday School, Reaching Adults Through the Sunday School, Reaching Youth Through the Sunday School, Reaching Children Through the Sunday School, Reaching Preschoolers* (resource kits also are available for each of these books), *Training Sunday School Workers in Outreach* (a Church Training Equipping Center planned especially for training *all* workers and members in outreach), *Training Outreach Workers for the Sunday School* (designed for training outreach leaders), *Adult Class Administration Kit, Adult Class Prospect Visitation Kit,* and *Youth Are Witnesses, Too Packet.*

Planning also is an essential part of the outreach program. The department workers should meet weekly to plan and coordinate outreach activities and assignments. These sessions should be led by the person responsible for outreach in the department and should take place during the weekly workers' meeting. The outreach director of the Sunday School checks on outreach activities and assignments by departments and classes. He also secures and evaluates reports and records of the activities and visits that have occurred. The weekly planning may be done at general sessions of the workers' meeting. Once a month, all outreach leaders should meet together during the teaching-learning segment of the weekly workers' meeting. Adult class outreach leaders should be included in this monthly meeting. This meeting should be scheduled so as not to interfere with Preschool and Children's departments' unit or monthly planning, usually done on Wednesday preceding the first Sunday of the month.

Maintaining Outreach Records

Outreach records should be kept and used to evaluate and plan outreach activities. Otherwise, Sunday School leaders are doomed to repeat nonproductive and discouraging activities. Sunday School workers should use outreach records to evaluate and improve their work.

Records may be used also to evaluate contacts and visits made. The records are a source of much information regarding who is making visits and contacts and who is not making them. Records reveal who are not being visited and contacted so that assignments can be made. The records also reveal the prospects' response to the contacts made. A Sunday School should be reporting each week a number of visits and contacts approximately equal to attendance.

Teachers' use of outreach records.—Teachers can use records to evaluate the effectiveness of their teaching. If only a few people are visiting in an Adult class, there is need for teaching about the biblical imperative of going. If only a few contacts are being made, there may be a lack of enthusiasm and a need for teaching on the outreach mission of the church. The absence of unsaved people on the rolls of Adult or Youth classes indicates a need to focus attention on reaching out to non-Christians and a need to enroll people in Bible study. The presence of unsaved people on the class roll or among the parents of preschoolers or children enrolled indicates opportunity for sharing evangelistic truths through personal witnessing and Bible teaching. Attendance and visitation records indicate the level of interest each member has in Bible study.

Outreach director's use of outreach records.—The outreach director of the Sunday School will use records to evaluate the effectiveness of outreach in the Sunday School. Numerous unsaved persons on the Sunday School rolls indicate that a reaching attitude and spirit exists. A large number of visits made suggests effectiveness of outreach leaders. A small number of professions of faith may indicate a need for increased emphasis on training in personal witnessing. If only a few new members are being enrolled, there is a need for increased emphasis on enrolling persons. Results of visits and contacts indicate areas where training and motivation are needed. Examination of the attendance records will show where there is need for increased emphasis on contacting persons regarding attendance. Enrollment records reveal whether departments and classes are accepting responsibility for reaching their assignments. Visitation records indicate also whether proper assignments are being made for enlistment, evangelism, and ministry in all age groups.

Moreover, frequent examination of the records will help the director determine whether adequate visitation records are being maintained and used for effective outreach.

Discovering Prospects

In many churches, Sunday School leaders do not know their outreach potential. They do not know who their prospects are. They do not know who is unsaved and who is unenlisted. If a church is to discover persons who should be reached, it must want to do so and it must decide to do so.

Discovering prospects means finding out who need to be reached with the gospel and for Bible study, where contact can be made, and what age group is responsible. It requires that the name, address, phone number, age, and spiritual condition of unsaved and unenlisted persons be known. In a prospect discovery system, the following actions may be taken:

1. Examine the church roll to discover church members not enrolled in Sunday School.

2. Get information about visitors in Sunday School, worship services, and other church activities.

3. Conduct a People Search (census).

4. Subscribe to newcomer lists.

5. Use ACTION and Mini-ACTION programs.

6. Identify prospects among Vacation Bible School participants and their families.

7. Identify prospects among Backyard Bible Club participants and their families.

8. Identify prospects among fellowship Bible class members and their families.

9. Identify prospects among Cradle Roll members and their families.

10. Identify prospects among Mission Vacation Bible School participants and their families.

11. Identify prospects among church bus riders and their families.

12. Take an inside census. That is, ask your members to provide information on their families' spiritual condition.

13. Use referrals from Home Bible Study referral service.

14. Use direct mail in prospect discovery.

15. Ask members to provide information on acquaintances, friends, associates, and other persons who are unreached. Urge them to include in their lists persons with special needs who may otherwise be overlooked—blind, deaf, mentally retarded, per-

sons with physical handicaps that make Sunday School attendance difficult, and persons who speak little or no English.

16. If the church has a recreation program, get prospect information from registration records of participants.

17. Watch the newspaper for new births.

18. Observe houses that have recent new occupants. Visit them even before newcomer lists are received.

Building and Using Prospect Files

Many churches have no record of prospects, no record of persons who visited Sunday School and worship services, and no newcomer list. Such a situation almost precludes the possibility of effective outreach. A prospect file is not difficult to set up and maintain. It can be done in any size church or mission. It can be managed with volunteer or paid help. It does take persistence and hard work. Misinformation is as bad as no information; it can sound the death knell to visitation.

A prospect filing system provides a permanent record of accurate information on prospects and makes this information available for use in assigning responsibility for making contact. Two plans are described below.

PLAN 1

People Search or family census file.—Usually filed by family name, each card in the file should record information about each member of the family (name, age, address, phone, and spiritual condition). On the card indicate the department or class to which each person has been assigned. This file is maintained by the outreach director, a church staff member, or by a person so designated.

Church office age-group prospect file.—This file also is the responsibility of the outreach director or a staff member. From the family file, individual prospect slips (Form 120) are prepared in triplicate. The originals are filed by classes and departments. This file remains in the church office. The duplicates are used by department and classes.

Class/department prospect file.—The duplicate copies of Form 120 are given to the appropriate department outreach leader. One copy is retained by the department outreach leader to form a department file, and the other copy is used for prospect visitation and cultivation assignment to workers and members.

PLAN 2

A Reach Out Prospect Assignment Pocket and Card is prepared for each prospect and filed in a class or department outreach notebook. This is used to give assignments to members or workers for making contacts with prospects and recording results of that contact. These cards can be placed in the card covers (Sunday School Record, Form 107-S) containing the class or department members' cards (Member's Record, Form 105-S). If this plan is used, however, it is important that the family census file be maintained for it becomes the master file.

Prospect Forms Available

The following forms are available: People Search Family Card, Prospect File Card (Form 5), Visitation Assignment (Form 3), Enrollment Prospect Visitation Assignment and Report (Form 120), Prospect Assignment Pocket and Card, and Personal Record Folder for Teachers and Leaders. The Prospect Assignment Pocket and Card is listed on the Undated Materials Order Form. The others are available from Baptist Book Stores.

Assigning Responsibility for Outreach

Perhaps you have discovered hundreds of prospects, have an impressive set of prospect files, and have organized and trained your workers. Now assignments must be made.

The church outreach director determines the responsibility for reaching prospects, according to the age of each prospect, and assigns prospects to the proper class or department. The proper prospect card is given to each department outreach leader. In small churches without department structure, assignments are made to the classes.

In Adult departments, the department outreach leader assigns prospects to proper classes through the class outreach leader.

The Youth department outreach leader uses the outreach prospect file to make assignments to teachers who, in turn, work with the class leaders in making assignments to members of the classes.

The director in Preschool departments and the department outreach leader in Children's departments use the outreach department prospect file to make assignments to workers for visits to be made. In each case, the person making the assignment for visitation should receive the report back from the person making the contact. The report back is as essential as the assignments were.

Visiting, Contacting, and Enrolling Prospects

The assignment has been made, but the purpose is that workers and members visit and enroll people in Sunday School. Successful visitation and outreach involve all Sunday School workers and members.

Visits are made for a variety of reasons: to enlist and enroll persons in Bible study, to win persons to Christ (treated more fully in chapter 9), to minister to them, and to encourage them to attend. The major thrust in outreach is made through personal visits in the homes, phone calls, cards, and letters. Daily contacts during the course of your work also are outreach opportunities. Sharing with neighbors and associates at home or at school is vital to outreach.

Now how are specific assignments made to members and workers?

The outreach director will make assignments on the weekly visitation day or days of the church. The visits will be made during the assigned time for visitation or at a later time, if necessary.

To supplement weekly visitation, which is absolutely essential, and to involve the largest possible number of workers and members, assignments are made by the department or class outreach leaders on Sunday morning in classes or departments or at the weekly workers' meeting, or both. Thus, visitation may be done any time during the week, as well as on visitation day. Growing churches almost without exception observe one or more definite weekly visitation days.

The monthly outreach workers' meeting, during part of the weekly workers' meeting, is a time for sharing prospect information.

Is there a plan for enrolling people in Bible study?

Absolutely! Open enrollment is strongly advocated. Open enrollment means enroll anyone, anytime, anywhere, providing the person agrees to be enrolled.

The idea that persons need to come three times in a new class before being enrolled is self-defeating. It is not promoted by denominational Sunday School leaders. Persons should be enrolled when they want to be enrolled.

Following enrollment, members should be assigned to the proper age-graded class or department.

Persons should be dropped from the roll only when they have died, moved away, or joined another Sunday School. When a person is removed from a roll, that person is often forgotten. The name of a chronic absentee on a roll is not harmful to the class and may serve as an outreach reminder. Let's be concerned personally about all people, their spiritual condition and needs.

Reporting on Assignments Received

Reporting on contacts and visits made means reporting information in usable form to the Sunday School office in a systematic and orderly way for future reference. The prospect assignment cards are used for these reports. Age-group workers and Adult group leaders and class outreach leaders should see that visitation information is recorded on the assignment slips or cards. The cards are given to the department outreach leader for transfer of information to the department prospect file, and the information is given to the person who keeps the general age-group file (outreach director, staff member, volunteer). These cards thus become available to the pastor and staff for reference. They are available to the outreach director for use in making further assignments and for sharing information on families of prospects with the appropriate departments.

The Preschool, Children's, or Youth department outreach leader collects reports of contacts on Sunday and delivers a summary report to the outreach director.

The report of total contacts is obtained by the Adult class outreach leaders and by the department outreach leaders of the other age groups for verbal reports or records from the class secretary. These reports are given to the outreach director of the Sunday School as part of the report summary.

Sustaining Members Through Outreach

Sunday School workers should be regularly in touch with the members of their department. Some workers contact their members every week. It is unthinkable that an absentee not be contacted with frequency. When one is absent from Sunday School, what does it mean? It can indicate sickness, death in the family, an emergency, a spiritual problem or need, indifference, or anger. Any one of these reasons indicates spiritual need. What do we do with those who have spiritual needs? We love them, comfort them, encourage them, and do whatever it takes to help them.

What form of contact is best with members? Usually the personal visit is the best, but telephone calls are of untold value. A personal letter is one of the best ways to minister. The important thing is that concern is expressed and felt.

VISITATION IS EXCITING

Visitation does pay! Visitation will work! Visitation is exciting! Visitation is exciting when there is a visitation program and plan. Does your church have a visitation program? Do you have new prospects? Do you know who they are and where they live? Is your visitation day once a week? every other week? Or do you visit as you can? The latter is not usually an effective visitation plan. In an effective visitation program, there is a definite time of assignment, a definite place of assignment, definite persons assigned, definite report, and definite follow-up.

Visitation is exciting when we really care about people, when we genuinely want to help them and minister to their needs. Visitation is exciting when the individual to be reached is at the center. Visitation is exciting when the Sunday School begins to see the possibilities for carrying out the concerns of Christ as it ministers. When we look beyond self and our own needs, visitation is exciting!

Visitation is exciting when we see new ideas being used; when we see new approaches and positive results; and when we look at the possibilities for new ways of reaching, enrolling, loving, and caring.

Visitation is exciting when all the Sunday School workers are involved, when all catch the vision and see the challenge. Visitation is exciting when the members see that they can have a part, too.

Visitation is exciting when we share failures and successes, joys and sorrows, and when we can sense *koinonia* and the shared Christian experience.

And visitation is exciting when the Holy Spirit is in control— when we let him lead, when he directs our efforts. Yes, visitation is exciting!

REACHING IS BEING DONE!

Reaching is taking place in Southern Baptist Sunday Schools across the nation. Al Allen, pastor of the Moose Creek Baptist Church, in North Pole, Alaska, talks enthusiastically about how prayer, planning, training, and work are keys to growing a church.

But it was not always so.

When Allen became pastor at Moose Creek, in May 1977, the Sunday School enrollment had declined to 31. Three months later, it had plummeted further to 22, and Allen was on his knees.

After surveying the Sunday School classes and finding only about 15 people present on the first Sunday in August 1977, Allen said he was so discouraged that he went to his office to pray.

"As I was praying, I guess I even had doubts about my calling," he said. "I made a commitment to do whatever the Lord wanted me to do. I believed if I was called there, there should be growth."

In the worship service that followed his commitment, seven families joined the church.

With a renewed sense of enthusiasm, the church set an attendance goal of 50, reaching it in September 1977.

Allen began to read everything he could find on church growth and Sunday School organization. He studied the growth patterns of his church. Based on information gleaned from his study, Allen determined that he would work to train the people and to enlarge the Sunday School. The result was that on some Sundays the number of people present and participating in Bible study was higher than the enrollment.

By the time a team from Louisiana arrived in April 1978 to conduct an ACTION campaign, the attendance at Moose Creek was averaging 125.

"On the day we started the ACTION program, twenty of our people showed up to work with the team," Allen said. "They had never gone visiting, never knocked on a door to share about the Lord Jesus Christ or invite someone to Sunday School."

Eighteen months later, following ACTION, starting a pastor's Bible study class, conducting three Vacation Bible Schools, and beginning the use of the Growth Spiral, the enrollment had reached 400, with an average attendance of 200.

As Allen looks back on the past two years, he cites attention to the Sunday School as a vital factor in the growth. "If we're going to grow a church, it has to start with the Sunday School program," he said.

Reaching people is happening in Ferguson, Missouri. Bob Werner, pastor of the First Baptist Church in Ferguson, has some penetrating insights about growing Sunday Schools. Werner said that he has been converted to the conviction that giving first priority to the Sunday School is the best way to grow a church.

Formerly, he had emphasized dynamic, celebrative worship, using many special guests. The results were positive—the church grew rapidly with the Sunday School enrollment doubling from 500 to 1,000 in four and one-half years.

When the growth leveled off, though, Werner and the staff began an evaluation process to identify possible causes. Their conclusion: "We didn't have a support system under the growth."

"I began to see that one of the dynamics of church growth is emphasizing cell growth," Werner said. "When a church grows on the basis of Sunday School classes locked into Bible study, it will continue to grow and reach more people."

With that conclusion, on September 13, 1979, Bible study was adopted as a priority, to be implemented beginning October 1.

Werner soon learned, however, that implementing the new priority would involve change, some of it painful. "When you make a decision to prioritize the Sunday School, it is going to cost you something," he said; "but the cost is worth it."

One of the costs at the Ferguson church involved changing an established policy concerning the two worship services. The services had been planned to be identical so that the television crew, made up of church members, could tape both services and choose the better product for their weekly thirty-minute program.

Now, different choirs and music groups are used in each service and the television crew tapes only one service so that everyone can attend Sunday School.

With the new priority implemented less than three months, Werner said that he already can see results. Sunday School attendance is averaging 199 more per week than in the same period of the previous year.

He quotes statistics unapologetically: "Numbers represent people, and Jesus said, 'Go after the people.' We've almost apologized as Southern Baptists for emphasizing numbers."

Reaching people for Bible study as well as worship has had another result in the Ferguson church. "We've got unsaved adults enrolled in Sunday School for the first time in years," said Werner, who expects to see many of these persons become Christians through their participation in weekly Bible study.

"You can have a revival a month and it won't do as much good as giving priority to the Sunday School," he added.

For the future, he said that the church needs both a new sanctuary and additional educational space. An educational building will come first because Sunday School is the priority. "There is no substitute for building a church through the Sunday School," he concluded.

---

[1]H. Cornell Goerner, *All Nations in God's Purpose* (Nashville: Broadman Press, 1979), p. 12.
[2]Ibid., p. 85.
[3]Ibid., p. 85.
[4]Ibid., p. 96.

Chapter 8

The Sunday School Is . . . Teaching People the Bible

"They received the message with great eagerness, studying the scriptures every day to see whether it was as they said. Many of them therefore became believers" (Acts 17:11-12, NEB).

When people are enrolled in Sunday School, they are taught the Bible—God's revelation to men. It is important to note that we teach the Bible to *persons*. We must recognize that each person learns and responds individually. The effective teacher knows that the only power in his teaching is from the Holy Spirit. *This chapter explores the exciting possibility of teaching persons the Bible in the power of the Holy Spirit.*

TEACHING STARTS WITH PERSONS
The Meaning of Personality

Man is a creation of God and made in the image of God, both morally and spiritually. Man is, therefore, more than a physical being; he is a spiritual being. Perhaps it is best to say that he has the capacity for developing his spiritual dimension. W. T. Conner wrote, "The greatest thing about man is not what he is, but it is what he is capable of becoming."[1] Man has the ability to think, to know, to reason, to reflect, to arrive at conclusions. He has the capacity to exercise will. He can make choices and form ideals. "Within the range of his heredity and environment, he has power of choice sufficient to make him a responsible moral agent."[2]

Though man's freedom is limited by heredity and environment, "this freedom is enhanced when man comes into conscious fellowship with God in Christ."[3]

Man is an emotional being. He can respond to himself, to others, and to God. This unique capacity to feel is seen at its best when man moves from sin into fellowship with God. The capacity for love is best seen in the cross of Christ.

Man has a moral nature. That is to say, each person possesses a sense of right and wrong. This moral nature, this sense of right and wrong, "comes to both the race and the individual by a creative act of God."[4]

Of course, man's capacities as a spiritual person are absolutely essential to an experience with Christ. This is so, because only "as an intelligent and free being, with power to know and choose, can man respond to and accept the gospel of Christ. Only as a being with a moral nature capable of knowing right from wrong with capacity to love God and man, can he live the life required by the gospel."[5]

It should be pointed out also that there is something in man that reaches out for the spiritual and the eternal. Man does indeed hunger and thirst for God. That longing was present in the days of the psalmist (Ps. 42:1). There are evidences everywhere that the longing is strong in the hearts of contemporary men and women. And this seeking after God is met only in Jesus Christ (John 14:6).

The Varieties of Personalities

Scientists tell us that of all the snowflakes that flutter to the earth, no two are alike. Far more significant, there are more than four billion human beings on this earth today, and yet, there are not two human beings exactly alike. Each of the four billion plus is different from all others. Each person is different physically and in personality and temperament. Each individual is unique.

This simple truth has significance for Sunday School workers. The teacher who really understands this truth seeks to teach each individual member of the class. The teacher will see each person as a unique personality with distinctive needs. The discerning teacher will see this truth in regard to unsaved and unenlisted persons. They are won to Christ one by one. This is the reason for classes and departments being small enough for individuals to receive personal concern, witness, and ministry. The uniqueness and variety of personality is one of the glories and mysteries of creation.

The Importance of Persons in the Bible

Not only is each person unique and made in the image of God, but each one is important. There is not a single person created by the Father who is without value. That is the magnificent revelation of Jesus Christ. It is the meaning of the cross. Was there one person for whom Jesus Christ did not die? *Not one.* The "whosoever" of John 3:16 is all inclusive.

The focus of the Bible is on that truth. Over and over in his ministry, Jesus taught that each person is important. As he encouraged the twelve about their mission in the world, he said "Are not two sparrows sold for a penny? And not one of them will fall to the ground without your Father's will. But even the hairs of your head are all numbered. Fear not, therefore; you are of more value than many sparrows" (Matt. 10:29-31, RSV).

The three parables of grace in Luke 15—the lost sheep, the lost coin, and the lost son—clearly reveal the importance Jesus attached to one person. Comparing the lost sheep to a sinner, Jesus said "Just so, I tell you, there will be more joy in heaven over one sinner. . . ." (Luke 15:7, RSV).

The Challenge of Persons

I once knew a teacher who had the unique capacity of helping each child in the department feel that he was special. There was so much love, acceptance, security, trust, respect, and guidance shown by this teacher that if you took a child aside to ask, "Who is Mrs. Thomason's favorite friend in this department?" every child would have answered, "I am." The ability to treat individuals in this manner is God-given, but it can be received any time in life. You can ask for it at twenty-five or fifty-five years of age. With God's help, you can improve in your ability to make each child feel special. The importance of individuals requires that Sunday School workers give attention to the special needs of each age group.

Needs of preschoolers.—Preschoolers have many needs: independence, sense of trust, security, acceptance, love, self-control, guidance, self-respect.

Teachers and parents need to realize that the primary need in a young child's life is love. How can he feel accepted and secure unless he knows that there is unconditional love surrounding him at home and at church? Just as Christian adults count on Christ's love, regardless of their performance and behavior, a young child needs to feel that he is protected in a cocoon of love.

When love and acceptance are evident, security follows. This attitude enhances freedom in a department room as a child gains self-confidence. Another way of saying this is, "A child will obey you if he is aware of your unreserved love for him as a person of worth." Someone has said, "You can discipline any child who is your disciple."

If a child develops a sense of trust in adults who care for him, he is more likely to accept the Christian faith when he matures. Christlike adults make it easy for a young one to comprehend a loving, compassionate God who cares what happens to him personally.

It is frightening to realize that a child behaves the way he thinks we expect him to behave. If he thinks we expect him to disobey, he will. Here are some ways to increase a child's self-respect:

1. Talk with him.
2. Listen to him.
3. Commend him, if you can do so sincerely.
4. Participate in activities with him. For an infant or toddler, spend time alone with him.
5. Show him courtesy and respect. Say, "thank you," "excuse me," and "please."

Although preschoolers are dependent, they struggle at various ages to become independent. Teachers should allow each one to do as much for himself as he is capable of doing. This is another way of expressing indirectly: "I believe in you. You are capable."

In order to have a healthy and happy group situation, there must be control. Older preschoolers sometimes push to know the limitations, and an understanding teacher provides these boundaries, knowing that they add security.

Guidance varies according to the age of a child. Redirecting young preschoolers is an excellent way to offer guidance.

Needs of children.—Children from six to eleven years of age have developmental tasks all their own. During these years, they develop more fully their own identity. It is during these years that children grow in the areas of mental ability, social development, and physical ability. They are learning to apply what they learn to their relationship with their peers. People outside the family and institutions in the community play important roles in the socialization of the child.

To meet the needs of children, Sunday School teachers need to understand individual characteristics. Children six to eleven years of age usually are active, inquisitive, independent, challengeable, sensitive, considerate, complaining, rebellious, flexible, eager to be liked by friends of the same age, and anxious to please others.

The Sunday School can help meet basic needs of children by accepting each child as a unique person, creating a sense of security, providing opportunities for achievement, allowing independence, giving approval of the child as a person, allowing each child to grow at his own rate, and giving love.

If Sunday School teachers begin with the child and ask what he needs and what problems he must solve, then allow him adventure in learning, teachers and pupils will be off to a good beginning in learning.

Needs of youth.—Youth Sunday School is something done *with* youth, not something done *to* youth. Absorbing the guidelines listed below will help a worker serve effectively with youth in providing them satisfying Sunday School experiences.

1. Accept youth.
2. Be aware of youth developmental stages.
   a. Youth is a time of moving from childhood to adulthood.
   b. Youth is a time of searching for an identity.
   c. Youth look for role models.
   d. Youth are strongly influenced by peers.
   e. Youth look for meaningful relationships.
   f. Youth will test and experiment.
3. Know why youth come to Sunday School.
   a. Social involvement
   b. Peer group
   c. Parents' expectations
   d. Role model's encouragement
   e. Needs met
   f. Personal desire to grow spiritually
4. Be involved with youth beyond the Sunday morning experience.
5. Know the spiritual condition of each youth in your group.
6. Stay in touch with youth culture.
7. Trust in the abilities of youth to learn.
8. Help youth assume responsibility.
9. Remember that every youth needs affirmation.

The greatest spiritual development of youth will come when workers can help youth intersect life needs with the truths of the Bible.

Needs of adults.—Over 70 percent of the United States population are adults, age eighteen years and over. This overlooked majority in our nation deserves careful examination by the compassionate Sunday School leader. Adults, even though they may be mature physically, are still pilgrims and should continue maturing mentally, socially, and especially spiritually throughout the adult years.

Adults are not alike. Some adults are homebound, married and with children, never or formerly married, living in institutions, or temporarily away from home. In fact, there is an enormous diversity during these years that makes working with adults one of the most challenging areas of service. Every prospect, every member, is unique.

There are many ways to consider meeting the needs of adults in Bible study. We usually consider three major groups: young adults, ages eighteen through twenty-nine; median adults, ages thirty through fifty-nine or retirement; and senior adults, age sixty or retirement and up. Young adults face important challenges regarding education, vocational choice, marriage, and family responsibilities. Adults in the middle years are at a strategic time for personal and spiritual growth. In these years some adults face difficult experiences, such as loss of a mate, physical changes, and vocational adjustment. Senior adults undergo physical changes, yet their capacity for enjoying Bible study and Christian service may be the strongest of their lifetime.

The greatest need for adults is to know Christ as Savior and Lord in their lives. The simple fact is that most adults in our nation do not know Christ as personal Savior. The Bible is primarily an Adult book. The greatest number of unsaved persons are adults. Our Sunday Schools must place not less emphasis on other age groups but an ever-increasing emphasis on adults. Our mission is to enroll adults in Bible study, to witness to them about Christ, and to teach them his Word. When we reach adults, other members of the family will be reached.

TEACHING REQUIRES LEARNING
How Preschoolers Learn

Preschoolers learn through imitation.—A preschooler learns to do what he sees and hears others do. For example, Tom and Julie have been building with the blocks. Mr. Mitchell says: "It is time to put the blocks away. I'll help you." He sings, "I Can Help." Tom and Julie do likewise.

Preschoolers learn through curiosity.—A preschooler discovers people and the world around him. Mrs. Doubet placed fall leaves of different colors and shapes on the nature shelf. Melanie discovered the leaves and the magnifying glass. She looked closely at the leaves and found two leaves that were the same shape. She listened to the crunchy sound when she crumpled the dry leaves in her hand and wondered what made them crumple.

Preschoolers learn through repetition.—A preschooler develops skills and refinement of skills. When Mrs. Hughes finished reading the story from the book, Wesley said, "Read it again." With each reading Wesley learned something new.

Preschoolers learn by doing.—A preschooler learns independence by actually doing things for himself. The four-year-olds made butter. Mrs. Williams let each child taste the whipping cream. They took turns shaking the container and eagerly watched the butter form. They tasted the buttermilk and ate the butter on crackers. Mrs. Williams said, "Thank you, God, for milk and butter."

Preschoolers learn through play.—A preschooler learns to interpret how he feels and thinks about himself and others; he also discovers the world around him. Mr. Lee brought green beans for the nature area. Cindy and Steve enjoyed snapping the beans. Mr. Lee said: "God made these beans to grow in the garden. God sent the sunshine and the rain to help the green beans grow."

Preschoolers learn through satisfaction.—A preschooler becomes discouraged if he meets too many failures. There must be plenty of time to manipulate materials, experiment with them, and develop confidence in his ability to do things. Cynthia finishes a puzzle and puts it back in the puzzle rack. She feels good inside because she was able to complete the puzzle.

Preschoolers learn through relationships.—The preschooler acquires feelings and attitudes, concepts, facts, and information. Toddler Andy is looking at a picture of Mary holding Jesus when he was a baby. Mrs. Ashley says: "This is a picture of Jesus when he was a baby. I love Jesus. I love you too, Andy!"

Preschoolers learn through their senses.—A preschooler learns through seeing, hearing, touching, smelling, and tasting. The three-year-olds went outside. Each child gathered leaves, flowers, rocks, and blades of grass. They saw interesting tree bark, smelled fragrant flowers, touched smooth stones, heard birds singing, and made many other discoveries. Their teachers sang songs like "Running Through the Leaves" and shared Bible thoughts such as "The birds have nests."

How Children Learn

One task of the Sunday School is to teach the Bible. A Sunday School teacher of children will want to seek ways to teach God's Word.

Children need to be taught the Bible in order to gain some basic understandings:

- Know the God of the Bible.
- Develop solid foundation for salvation.
- Know the Christ of the Bible and experience him as Savior when they are ready.
- Make lifelong investments in high ideals.
- Learn and experience love.
- Learn from models after which they will want to pattern their lives.
- Know that the Bible is God's message to people.
- Know that God has commanded children to be taught the Bible.

These basic principles of learning are involved when a Sunday School teacher guides children in the study of God's Word. Teachers help children learn when teachers motivate children to want to know; when children enjoy themselves; when teachers relate what is being studied to things with which children are already familiar; when teachers create a need within children for the information included in the study; when teachers involve children in things in which they are interested; when teachers present material that has a logical order or relationship to the children's lives; when teachers provide examples for children to imitate; when there is repetition; when the senses are stimulated;

and when teachers involve children in the teaching-learning process.

An important factor in the children's learning situation is the Sunday School teacher. Teaching a child the truths of the Christian faith requires a teacher who can share these truths from personal experience.

How Youth Learn

The wise Sunday School director will recognize and trust in the ability of youth to learn.

Youth can learn.—A healthy respect for the ability of youth to learn Christian concepts is necessary for the effective Youth worker. Recognition of this ability will allow youth to explore ideas. Workers can still guide them as they reach conclusions and make decisions. Youth can know Christ as personal Savior and Lord. This is the greatest decision of life. All unsaved youth need this experience more than any other.

Youth must be motivated to learn.—Creating interest in the study is the first step in any learning experience. Few youth arrive at Sunday School with arms outstretched saying, "Here I am; I'm ready to learn." It is the responsibility of the Youth worker to relate to some need in a youth's life and tie that need into the study in such a way that the youth says to himself, "I need to know that!"

Youth learn by being involved.—This idea relates primarily to the need of youth to test and experiment. Coming face to face with the challenges and demands of the Bible and the Christ of the Bible is an exciting experience and one that any youth will enjoy.

Involving youth in various techniques of Bible study allows the worker and youth to explore the depth of God's message. Involving youth also acknowledges that the youth learning mechanism works the same way on Sunday as it does on Tuesday. Statistics prove to us that we learn more from what we *do* (are involved in) than what we *hear*.

How Adults Learn

Adults can learn and they do learn. Colleges and universities across our nation are filled with adults returning to school. It is a myth that adults cannot learn: adults learn as well as children and youth in most kinds of learning, but they are not always as quick in learning. They are better in concept learning. Adult learning is voluntary, and adults respond best to need-centered learning. Adult learning is best when it is relational.

Adults learn better when more senses are involved.—Of course, learning does take place when only hearing is involved. When sight is involved, additional learning takes place. When doing becomes involved in the process, greater learning is possible. This is the reason that posters, strip charts, and filmstrips are useful in the learning process.

Adults learn more in a pleasant, comfortable environment.—If there is adequate space, adult learning is more successful. Proper equipment, furnishings, and teaching tools are helpful also in the learning process.

Adults learn better when the study has meaning for their own lives.—If adults are shown and can see and feel that the Bible study has practical meaning for their lives, they are more apt to learn.

Adults learn better when various methods are used.— Sometimes the lecture is the best method to use in teaching adults. Sometimes, the case study is applicable. Thoughtful questions may be asked. Class discussion often is highly profitable. Listening teams may be formed. No method should be used all of the time. The best method is probably a variety of methods during each Bible study period.

Adults generally learn better when experience is involved.— Not all adults wish to share experiences or participate in Bible study activities, but many do. When they do, they improve their learning possibility, for the learning level is high when experience is involved.

Adults learn by example.—As in all age groups, the quality and

commitment of the life of the teacher helps or hinders the learning of the adults. Adults are inspired and encouraged to learn by the example of teachers and fellow learners.

TEACHING FOCUSES ON SCRIPTURE
The Bible as Textbook

J. M. Frost said, "The work of the Sunday School is threefold; First, teach the Scriptures; second, teach the Scriptures; third, teach the Scriptures."

Of course, he did not mean that teaching is the only purpose of the Sunday School, nor did he mean that Bible content alone is the purpose of teaching. He knew, and we know, that Bible content is to be taught, but there is no teaching until there is learning. If the Bible is really learned, then it is lived and applied. The Bible is the written witness of God's revelation to persons. Therefore, the Bible involves more than information; it involves the possibility for transformation when a person meets God through Holy Scripture. That person not only is informed; he is transformed.

The textbook of the Sunday School is the Bible. There is no other textbook. The Bible is the textbook of the Sunday School because it is the "inspired written record of God's revelation to men."[6] It is authoritative and it is final for us in "all the matters of our Christian faith and conduct."[7]

When we read the Old Testament, we observe often the phrase "Thus saith the Lord," particularly in the prophets. Jeremiah said, "The word of the Lord came unto me" (Jer. 1:4). The New Testament has numerous references regarding source. The apostle Paul wrote: "All scripture is given by inspiration of God" (2 Tim. 3:16).

The Bible tells us where we came from, who we are, and where we are going.

The Bible is the only book that reveals the way to salvation and life eternal. It speaks throughout the pages of God's redemptive purpose through Jesus. "The Bible points forward to Christ, backward to Christ, and again forward to Christ in his glorious return and reign."[8]

The Bible gives the pattern for human conduct (2 Tim. 3:16-17). It speaks to the basic issues of life. It is as up to date as today's newspaper. It is for the young and old. It tells how to live a Christlike life.

The Bible is a book of comfort and hope. It provides courage and strength in time of need.

The Bible contains truth which, when applied, will mold and develop individual Christian character and produce Christian homes of enduring quality.

Curriculum Materials as Support

Curriculum materials are support for the Bible study session—no more or no less. The foundation of all Southern Baptist church curriculum materials rests implicitly on the Bible and its nature and message. The publishing of printed materials is to aid the churches in the fulfilling of their mission. Bible study materials are published to assist the Sunday School in its reaching, teaching, witnessing, and ministering tasks. Curriculum materials can never be considered a substitute for a study of the Bible. Bible study materials are prepared to provide for each age group a systematic plan of study and to provide tools for learning for both teachers and pupils. They are designed to help persons understand, appreciate, and apply the Bible in their daily lives.

The preparation of printed materials is a complex process, requiring a great deal of planning and coordination. Here are the basic guidelines followed by those persons who design the Sunday School's Bible study materials:

1. The Bible is at the heart of the design process. All materials must faithfully reflect the message of the Bible in a clear and compelling manner.

2. Materials must be doctrinally sound, reflecting beliefs common to Southern Baptists. The most recent statement outlining these common beliefs is *The Baptist Faith and Message* state-

ment adopted by the Southern Baptist Convention on May 9, 1963. In addition, all writers of curriculum materials are committed Southern Baptists.

3. Suggestions for teaching and implementation must be educationally sound and must consider both the developmental needs of the age group for which they are written and the persistent life needs common to all persons.

4. Materials must be practically usable by the widest possible majority of Southern Baptist churches. For example, a teaching procedure not only must be educationally sound, but it also must call for resources and skills readily available to most Southern Baptist churches.

5. Materials should be well written from a literary standpoint and should be attractive in format and appearance. Evaluations from persons who use our materials are often helpful in determining how these materials can be produced and used more effectively.

6. Developers of materials try to take into consideration basic days in the Christian calendar, such as Christmas and Easter, that are dear to Southern Baptists. In addition, materials are planned to reflect and undergird special denominational emphases, such as Bold Mission Thrust, and ongoing emphases, such as evangelism.

7. Curriculum materials produced by the Sunday School Board must be designed to help accomplish the overarching educational objective of the church which is: To help persons become aware of God as revealed in Scripture and most fully in Jesus Christ, respond to him in a personal commitment of faith, strive to follow him in the full meaning of discipleship, relate effectively to his church and its mission in the world, live in conscious recognition of the guidance and power of the Holy Spirit, and grow toward Christian maturity.

TEACHING REQUIRES THE PROPER SETTING

Learning is significantly affected by the setting. The setting is considered as the space, equipment, and furnishings provided in a class or department room.

Learning is influenced by the provision or lack of provision of space needed. Adequate provision of space is important not because it ensures learning, but, rather, because it makes learning possible.

Proper furnishings, equipment, and tools also influence the learning-teaching setting. Furnishings are those items usually selected by special furnishings committees assigned the responsibility. These items usually are movable and can easily be interchanged from room to room. Chairs, tables, chalkboards, maps, and the like are considered furnishings.

Equipment usually is mentioned in nature and specified in the architect's plan and normally installed by the contractor. Equipment items are affixed to the building and are considered part of the structure.

Tools are such items as chalkboards, pictures, posters, filmstrips, and slides.

Setting for Preschool Learning

Preschoolers are active by nature. Therefore, they need space to move about and develop their mind, body, and muscles commensurate with their maturation.

Because preschoolers have such a short-attention span, they need a variety of materials that challenge their thinking and develop their skills. A choice of materials for preschoolers to explore and discover helps them satisfy the need of curiosity.

Ideally preschoolers should have a rectangular shaped room, a room that is three-fourths as wide as it is long. Generally, the room for preschoolers should be at least 15 by 20 feet.

It usually is a good idea to locate Preschool departments as near as possible to Young Adult departments to improve the traffic flow within the church building. It is easier for a young couple to take their preschooler to his department and then move to their department. The Preschool department should be located near an outside door, and near a water fountain and rest room. Windows can provide opportunities for preschoolers to learn.

A room decorated with bold colors can distract young children from learning activities. Bold designs cause them to be aimless in their direction. The best learning environment consists of softly colored walls and floors.

Babies, creepers, and toddlers need a quiet environment, which is conducive to rest. Neutrals and soft pastels are good wall colors for this age group. Blue has a calming and relaxing effect on young preschoolers. Soft blue light even has been found to make infants cry less.

A Preschool room should be large enough to allow at least twenty feet per child—preferably, twenty-five or more. Where space is limited, a minimum of furnishings should be used. Tables and chairs can be kept at a minimum, and an Autoharp or record player can replace the piano. If necessary, plan to have one activity in the hallway or outside, weather permitting. Open shelves are recommended, but materials may be placed on a window ledge or even in a corner on the floor.

Space assigned to preschoolers is space that is important for a church's educational program. Compare your department room arrangement with the suggestions that are made in chapter 8 of *Basic Preschool Work*. Notice the equipment that is suggested and the arrangement of the furnishings in the room.

Setting for Children's Learning

The rooms in which Children's workers teach are silent partners in the teaching-learning process. They can make learning a much happier and more effective process. Or, they can handicap both teacher and learner. There is no way to escape the fact that department rooms influence learning.

A department room without classrooms is the best type of space for a Children's department, but this arrangement is not always available. The recommended amount of space in a Children's department room is twenty-five square feet of floor space for each person enrolled. Since the recommended maximum enrollment for a Children's department is thirty, the largest room needed is 25 feet by 30 feet long.

Applying this rule to a small enrollment would indicate that only 250 square feet would be needed for a department of ten, including workers and pupils. But be careful: furnishings and equipment require virtually the same amount of space even though enrollment is far below the recommended maximum. And note this limitation: such a small room would allow no room for growth.

So what minimum size should be considered when a church provides new space? In view of all the factors involved, no Children's department room should be less than 20 feet wide by 24 feet long.

For further details on equipment and arrangement of Children's departments, see *Basic Children's Sunday School Work*, chapter 12.

Setting for Youth Learning

Here are some ideas for creating a learning environment for Youth Sunday School work.

1. Provide a minimum of eight to ten square feet of space per person in department room (or open rooms), based on 70 percent of the enrollment.

2. Provide a minimum of ten to twelve square feet per person in classroom, based on 70 percent of the enrollment. Classrooms should be no smaller than 10 by 12 feet but need not be uniform in size.

3. Provide adequate amount of supplies: literature, records, study books, hymnals, paper, art supplies, and other study materials.

4. Provide adequate furnishings: tables, chairs, resource center, musical instruments, and lapboards.

For details on youth learning setting, see chapter 8 in *Basic Youth Sunday School Work*.

Does total-period teaching require open-room teaching? This question often is asked in Youth Sunday School conferences. The answer is never simple. Total-period teaching does not mean you *have* to use open-room teaching; however, total-period teaching does *allow* for open-room teaching for those workers who prefer it.

Total-period teaching can be accomplished in any space—open room or in the traditional department and classroom space.

Leaders should survey space and analyze how workers feel about the issue. Open-room teaching is not for everyone. It is threatening to some workers. In such cases, departments would maintain permanent class groupings in open space.

Setting for Adult Learning

The environment where adults meet for Bible study greatly affects Adult learners and their learning experiences. Walls and floors convey messages! They give the feeling that something is going on, that people are at work, that conclusions are being made. There should be adequate ventilation, nonglare lighting, acoustical ceiling, appealing colors on the walls, and carpet on the floor.

Each Adult department room should provide eight to ten square feet per person expected in attendance. The classroom should have ten to twelve square feet of floor space for each person.

Furnishings for the department room should include movable chairs, movable chalkboards, a small table for the secretary, piano, coatrack, and storage space. The focal wall should be left blank or have a tackboard so that resource kit items and other visual aids can be displayed.

Furnishings for the classroom should include movable chairs, a table for the teacher, Bible maps, chalkboard, and a blank wall or tackboard for the focal wall.

At least once a year, the department director and teachers should evaluate the learning setting for adults, using the information in the preceding paragraphs. Then they should decide what improvements are needed and how they can be made.

For more details on the setting for Adult learning, see chapter 3 and Appendix in *Basic Adult Sunday School Work*.

WHEN THE IDEAL IS NOT AVAILABLE

The responsibility to teach and provide learning experiences is an ongoing responsibility of a church. This responsibility must be assumed regardless of the church's ability to provide the ideal setting.

Setting Isn't Everything

A loving, caring teacher who has prepared to share the riches of God's truth can find a group of learners ready to learn. The setting or environment, apart from teacher and learners, will not be limiting when these attitudes exist. The spirit and unity of the group can bring about a warm fellowship even in an uncomfortable room. People may be willing to sacrifice comfort and attractiveness for a feeling of being wanted, loved, and appreciated.

In many churches, the choices referred to above do not have to be made. There are ways and means, even in the smallest church or the church least financially able, to have more attractive and comfortable facilities and furnishings.

Improving or Adapting What Is Available

The first step in improving or adapting space is to recognize what is appropriate and what is inappropriate with the space, facility, and furnishings presently available. Chapter 12 of the *Sunday School Director's Handbook* provides information about the proper use of space. The Church Architecture Department of the Sunday School Board can help with a space analysis, based on the organizational structure and needs of the church program organizations. Also, each state convention has a church building consultant who can help.

Once space needs have been determined, a decision must be

made concerning the location of departments and classes within the space available. The following questions concerning altering and upgrading the present facility must be answered:

• What adjustments can be made to fit the present and future organization in the space available?

• Can alterations be made by people within the congregation or will a contractor be needed to do the work?

• Is money available in the budget for materials and labor required?

• If not, could the money be secured?

• When can the work be done in order to create the least amount of confusion for present occupants?

• Will the church property and space committee make decisions about remodeling? If not, who in the church will be responsible for planning and seeing that the work is done correctly and on schedule?

Remodeling to upgrade.—There are basically three things that influence prospects and members to want to return frequently to participate in Bible study: the warmth and spirit of the group, the effectiveness of the teacher, and the facility where the group meets. The last of these three has a far greater impact than may be imagined. An attractive, comfortable room can make the difference in whether there is continuing involvement in the Bible study group.

In seeking to upgrade present facilities, take advantage of the opportunity to correct the most common problems found in church buildings, such as these:

• Improper or insufficient lighting, both natural and artificial

• Heating and air conditioning inadequacies

• Space that is too small or too large for efficient use.

• Poor accessibility or traffic flow to and from related facilities

• Use of large open space for classes

• Acoustical problems caused by high ceilings, lack of sound absorbent materials, and thin uninsulated walls

• Floor covering that requires continuous maintenance

- Paint colors inappropriate to the age group or the intended use of the room

In securing a building permit for extensive remodeling, it is required in many areas to provide ramps or elevators for wheelchair members and prospective members so confined. This need must be considered in the planning stage of the remodeling project. This kind of upgrading increases the church's ability to reach out and to minister.

Upgrading may begin with just one room or one department. The leaders of other departments will be influenced and be desirous of improving the area where they work. A better approach, however, is to have a long-range plan that relates to the total facility, seeking to meet the needs of every group. The appropriate church committees should be involved in the planning.

Altering space to adapt.—The most common alteration done is the removal of a partition to make one good-sized room from two, both of which were too small for effective use. Sometimes the opposite may need to be done. If a group is using only one-half or less of a large room and future growth and organization do not project a need for the large room, it may be divided with a partition, providing for the addition of another unit organization. Both rooms should have doorways to a hallway.

Many churches have assembly and classroom areas where the Children's department meets. If the classroom walls are not weight-bearing walls, they may be removed and the total space divided into two open areas for use by two Children's departments. If it is not practical to remove partitions to classrooms, the doors may be removed to provide easy access to and from the large- and small-group areas.

When access to a department is through another department, there usually is room to build a partition down one side of the department area to form a hallway to the inaccessible area.

Making furnishings.—Nearly every church has one or more persons who have not only the skills but also the tools to make furnishings, especially those needed for Preschool and Children's groups. For diagrams of this furniture, secure *Make Your Own Preschool Furniture* (Code 9143-0), and *How to Build Equipment, Children's Departments, Grades 1 through 6* (Code 9251-1) on the Undated Materials Order Form from the Sunday School Board. It usually is inadvisable to make furniture for youth and adults. An exception may be tables. Avoid the use of benches and pews in the learning environment if at all possible.

Principles that stretch dollars.—Here are some tips that will help Sunday School leaders be good stewards of the money available.

- Always plan ahead.
- Secure quality products backed by reputable firms.
- Make alterations based on long-range plans.
- Make double use of space and furnishings.
- Remember that cheap price may mean poor quality.
- Use volunteer labor under capable supervision.
- Build facilities that have multiple uses.
- Use facilities for ethnic or language groups at alternate times.
- Have an energy conservation consciousness.
- Provide for the people; they will pay their own way.

TEACHING IS EMPOWERED BY THE HOLY SPIRIT

Given the best curriculum, the finest methods, well-defined organization, and the best space and equipment, success in teaching is not assured. One thing more is needful: the Holy Spirit. Teachers cannot, must not, teach in their own power. Without the leadership and guidance of the Holy Spirit, there is no power.

It is the "Christ in us"; it is the indwelling presence of the Holy Spirit that is responsible for every vestige of fruit. It is not because of our efforts or ingenuity. The apostle Peter made that clear when he wrote, "no prophetic message ever came just from the will of man, but men were under the control of the Holy Spirit as they spoke the message that came from God" (2 Pet. 1:21, TEV).

Let it be clear, the goal of Christian teaching is encounter—encounter with God, encounter with the living Christ—that leads to individual response. The teacher seeks to impart information. But that is not all. Information that leads to response and application—that is the goal.

---

[1] W. T. Conner, *Christian Doctrine* (Nashville: Broadman Press, 1937), p. 18.
[2] Ibid., p. 19.
[3] Ibid., p. 19.
[4] Ibid., p. 21.
[5] Ibid., p. 22.
[6] Herschel Hobbs, *The Baptist Faith and Message* (Nashville: Convention Press, 1971), p. 21.
[7] Ibid., p. 30.
[8] Ibid., p. 26.

Chapter 9

The Sunday School Is . . . Winning People to Christ

"You shall receive power when the Holy Spirit has come upon you; and you shall be my witnesses in Jerusalem and in all Judea and Samaria and to the end of the earth" (Acts 1:8, RSV).

As a general rule, a person is enrolled in a Sunday School class or department, then taught the Bible following enrollment. Next, the witness from a believer to an unbeliever usually occurs. It is not necessary, however, to force that order. A witness may be given on the first contact. In other words, sometimes enrollment and Bible study precede witness. Sometimes they do not. Sometimes the Holy Spirit leads in exactly the opposite way from that planned.

In any case, having dealt with reaching and teaching, we now consider the topic "Winning People to Christ." Witnessing is dealt with separately in order to give it proper focus, visibility, and significance.

THE IMPERATIVE TO WITNESS
Definition

It is imperative that a church witness. A Sunday School should be the witnessing organization of a church. The very definition of the word provides the key.

What does "witness" mean? A dictionary definition is "one who gives evidence of something that he has seen or heard." From a legal view, a witness is one who is called to testify before a court, to tell what took place. "Witness," as a verb, means to provide or serve as evidence of, to testify; to bear witness to what happened. This is the kind of witness made in a court of law. So "witness" is a courtroom word, which has a unique usage in the Christian faith. When we speak of a Christian witness, we think of a Christian's testimony or of his experience with Christ. When we think of a Christian witnessing, we think of that person sharing his faith and seeking to lead another person to Christ.

When referring to Sunday School, witnessing can be defined in this way: "It is the people of God actively seeking out unredeemed persons; sharing concern for them; teaching them God's truths through Bible study; and leading them, under the influence of the Holy Spirit, into a faith relationship with God through Jesus Christ."[1]

"Witness" is a biblical word. It is used of persons who made known to others their experiences of God's redemptive actions (Isa. 43:10,12; 44:8; Luke 24:48; Acts 1:8; 2:32; 3:15). Since many early Christians witnessed at the cost of their lives, the word for "witness" (*martees*) came to have the meaning "martyr" (Acts 22:20; Rev. 2:13). It is significant, also, that Hebrews 12:1 calls the Old Testament heroes of faith the "cloud of witnesses."

The Purposes of the People of God

The very nature and purpose of the people of God calls forth witnesses. Surely it is the purpose of his church to carry out the will of Christ in the world, and that will is that Christians proclaim and witness. Of course, it involves worship and teaching as well as proclamation and witness. The church cannot be the church unless it has a redemptive nature, for the church "grew out of the redemptive mission and work of Jesus Christ."[2]

The redemptive purpose of God is the central theme of the New Testament. The church would have to deny itself were it not to be a witnessing community. To the extent that a church fails to witness, it fails to be Christ's church.

The Evangelistic Message of the Bible

The Bible is crystal clear on this matter. Jesus himself came preaching, teaching, and calling for repentance and obedience (Mark 1:14-15). One of his first acts was to call for those persons who would share in his redemptive mission (Mark 1:16-20). Jesus taught his followers and then sent them out to give witness to the compassion and love of the Father (Matt. 10:5-15; Luke 9:1-6).

Following his resurrection, Jesus commanded his followers to be witnesses, to make disciples, and to teach the new converts to observe his teachings (Matt. 28:18-20; Luke 24:46-48; John 20:21; Acts 1:8). There could not be a more straightforward command! The message is clear. We are to go, and we do not go alone, for Jesus said, "Lo, I am with you alway, even to the end of the age" (Matt. 28:20, NASB).

The Witness Example of the Early Church

We noted earlier that the book of Acts clearly reveals a church empowered, emboldened, and guided by the Spirit—faithfully, prayerfully, and joyfully giving witness to a living Lord. The Bible records how that young church in its fervent witness literally turned its world upside down in a short time. Consider some New Testament examples of the early Christians' experiences in giving testimony to their Lord:

The witness of John the Baptist to Jesus (John 1:14-18)

Andrew leading his brother Simon to Jesus (John 1:41-42)

Philip leading Nathanael to Jesus (John 1:45-46)

Jesus' witness to Nicodemus (John 3)

Jesus' witness to the woman at the well (John 4:7-38)

Jesus' witness to an adulterous woman (John 8:2-11)

Jesus' witness to the man born blind (John 9:1-41)

Peter's witness at Pentecost (Acts 2:14-47)

Peter's and John's witness to the lame man and to the crowd in Solomon's portico (Acts 3:1-17)

Peter's witness before the Sanhedrin (Acts 4:5-22)

Peter's and the apostles' witness to the high priest (Acts 5:27-32)

The apostles' witness following their release (Acts 5:42)

Stephen's witness before the high priest (Acts 7)

The scattered believers' witness (Acts 8:4)

Philip's witness in Samaria (Acts 8:5)

Peter's witness to Simon the sorcerer (Acts 8:9-25)

Philip's witness to the Ethiopian eunuch (Acts 8:26-39)

Philip's witness in many towns (Acts 8:40)

Paul's witness in the synagogues following his Damascus experience (Acts 9:20-22)

Peter's witness to Aeneas (Acts 9:34-35)

Peter's witness at Joppa (Acts 9:36-42)

Peter's witness to Cornelius (Acts 10:34-43)

The disciples' witness at Antioch (Acts 11:19-26)

Paul's witness to the Ephesian elders (Acts 20:24)

Scriptures clearly reveal the direct and positive verbal witness that seemed to characterize the early church witness:

"But Peter and John answered and said to them, 'Whether it is right in the sight of God to give heed to you rather than to God, you be the judge; for we cannot stop speaking what we have seen and heard' " (Acts 4:19-20, NASB).

"Every day, in the temple and from house to house, they kept right on teaching and preaching Jesus as the Christ" (Acts 5:42, NASB).

"Therefore, those who had been scattered went about preaching the word" (Acts 8:4, NASB).

"Philip opened his mouth, and beginning from this Scripture he preached Jesus to him" (Acts 8:35, NASB).

"Those who were scattered because of the persecution that arose in connection with Stephen made their way to Phoenicia and Cyprus and Antioch, speaking the word to no one except to Jews alone. But there were some of them, men of Cyprus and Cyrene, who came to Antioch and began speaking to the Greeks also, preaching the Lord Jesus" (Acts 11:19-20, NASB).

The Responsibility of Each Believer

Each member of the church is responsible for witnessing. Some people feel that only a few should be involved in the witnessing of the church. They suggest that a limited number have the gift of witnessing. Such a position cannot be supported biblically. It is true that not all Christians and members of the church are equally skilled in this regard, nor are Christians equally committed. Every Christian, however, can and should have a personal and verbal witness as well as a life-style that is a witness. Each Christian has had a conversion as well as a continuing experience with Christ and, hence, has something to share. Because of what he has experienced he has a responsibility for and can grow in the attempt to lead others to know Jesus Christ as personal Savior and Lord. To think otherwise is to deny the clear teaching of Scripture.

The Condition of the Lost

Each person has a choice. Man is God's creation and bears his image (Gen. 1:27). As such, he possesses reason and has freedom of choice. Man was made for fellowship with God and has infinite value. Though created in the image of God, man deliberately chose to sin (Gen. 3) in his rebellion against God. Rebellion results in alienation from God. Therefore, man, as a sinner, needs forgiveness. Man cannot bridge the resulting gap and he cannot escape from his condemning sin. Jesus alone bridges that gap. God took the initiative in rescuing us, providing an escape, from our moral and spiritual ruin (John 3; Rom. 5:6-11; 2 Cor. 5:14-21).

God came to our rescue by his own Son's sacrificial death on the cross to take away our sin, to pay the price for our sin, to face our judgment for sin. Victory, however, came through the resurrection of Jesus Christ. New life is available to every person because of the cross and the resurrection. Unless, however, that redemptive message is heard, received, and accepted—unless Jesus Christ truly becomes Savior and Lord—there is not salvation and man is lost without hope.

The condition of a person, according to Christ, is clear. Jesus said, "I am the way, the truth, and the life; no one comes to the

Father but through me" (John 14:6, NASB). If one does not come to salvation through Jesus Christ, he will not be saved. There is no other way to be rightly related to God. The Bible speaks of only two places following death—heaven and hell, to be with God or to be separated from him. Those who are saved will be with Christ in heaven, and those who are lost will be without Christ in hell. Some persons are uncomfortable with this conclusion, but that is what God's Word says, and it is authoritative.

SEEKING THE LOST
Sensitizing Members to Be Aware of Unsaved Persons

Southern Baptists have been and still are known as "a people of the Book." We are an evangelistic people. We are a people who insist upon personal individual regeneration. We say that each person must individually experience Christ. We may do more "talking" than "walking," however, when it comes to witnessing and sharing Christ. We talk about evangelism and church growth, but do we really witness and share our faith regularly? We seem almost lulled to sleep by an inflated growth in finances, additional buildings, and transfers by letter. We appear to have an illusion of growth. Let's look at the kinds of church growth. They are (1) transfer growth; (2) biological growth; and (3) conversion growth.

Transfer growth occurs when new members are received by transfer of membership. Biological growth comes when members of church families are saved. Conversion growth is realized when new Christians come from the 130-160 million unsaved in our nation who have no relationship to church members. That is, they are not biologically related. Many churches know that there are large numbers of unsaved and unchurched persons, but they do not seek aggressively to win them to Christ. There is a temptation to become self-satisfied; to be status-quo-oriented; to think that if they "hold their own," they are doing well. Churches and Sunday Schools become maintenance-minded because they can see transfer growth and biological growth, but they are unaware that conversion growth is not present. Thus, an illusion of growth is created. It is a saddening and tragic fact that 6,191 Southern Baptist churches did not baptize a single person in 1978-79. This is another indication of the absence of conversion growth.

Many churches and Sunday Schools use most of their budget, calendar, and leadership in maintenance activities. They spend most of their efforts in reaching and ministering to the members of the church and Sunday School and too little in reaching out to the lost and unchurched. Thus, this illusion of growth results in complacency, apathy, inertia, and self-satisfaction.

Not all churches are in this position. Some are training Sunday School workers and members to witness to people who are not Christians and to enroll them in Bible study. They have a strong personal commitment to the Great Commission. They believe that the first business of the church is to find and lead these unsaved persons to Christ and to do everything possible to help them grow as disciples. Among these witnessing congregations are churches of all sizes and in all locations and areas. They are intensely serious about winning people to Christ. For them, nothing has higher priority. More and more churches are beginning to get involved in this commitment.

Being aware of the need for witness and becoming concerned about the lost are preliminaries to having a growth sensitivity. We must begin to think conversion growth—to think reaching, teaching, and winning people. We must commit, we must act. Waiting won't do it. Good intentions are not helpful. Witnessing and winning take commitment, hard work, and prayer. When these things are happening, there is no illusion of growth.

Planning Ways to Locate Unsaved Persons

Ways of locating people were listed in chapter 7. Now we zero in on special means of locating those who are unsaved.

Search class and department rolls.—Nearly every church has some Sunday School members who are not members of any church. They probably are unsaved. There are more unsaved children and youth than unsaved adults in our Sunday Schools. In fact, in most churches there are few unsaved adults enrolled in Sunday School. This is a tragic situation, for there are millions of adults in our nation who are UNSAVED. They need Jesus Christ as Savior and Lord.

Churches should constantly seek to enroll more unsaved persons in their Sunday Schools, and among these should be unsaved adults from all life-styles and the entire adult age range.

The plain truth is that if we expect to make significant advances in leading people to Christ, we must find and enroll unsaved adults and youth in Bible study.

Carefully analyze visitor cards.—If churches will ask for needed information at various activities of the church, they will discover unsaved persons. For instance, note the following possibilities for securing such information:

• Regular worship services—every Sunday morning and evening
• Wednesday night services
• Sunday School classes
• Training groups
• Special music concerts
• Recreation activities, particularly if a church has a family life center or a recreation building
• Day school or kindergarten
• Socials, fellowships, or retreats

People really will provide such information, but it must be requested.

Use the circle of influence approach.—Every person has friends, family, and various other relationships. Lead members and workers to ask: Who are the people I associate with most? Who are the people I see occasionally? regularly? This is the circle of influence. One or more unsaved persons probably are in each person's circle. If so, they are potential Christians. Consider the potential if church members would seriously approach these persons. In this ever-widening circle are the friends and family of the new convert. The new Christian wants them to know of his experience and shares it. The circle widens again as friends and relatives of the new Christian accept Christ. Thus, the circle of influence grows. It has the ultimate ripple effect.

Listen to experiences of others.—If we will make it a point simply to listen closely to what others say, often we will discover a person is lost whom we thought was saved. It is, of course, a sensitive matter and we must be wise in approaching such a person. Many witness opportunities are available to each of us daily. We should prayerfully ask God's wisdom and guidance in each opportunity.

Conduct People Search.—Of course, conducting a house-to-house survey remains one of the best ways to locate unsaved persons. Because of the changing pattern of American life, it is more difficult to knock on a door and ask for information and witness, but it still is one of the finest ways to discover lost people.

SHARING CONCERN FOR THE UNREDEEMED
Training Persons to Witness

Members not only must feel constrained to witness, but they must be trained in witnessing. This training should take two forms. It should be the study of witnessing and the practice of witnessing. These two elements are combined beautifully in the Sunday School Evangelism Workshop approach. This event includes study, worship, information sharing, and the actual involvement of workers and members in faith-sharing visits to Sunday School members and prospects who are not Christians. It is based on the study course book *Witness to Win,* compiled by Max L. Caldwell. This book was designed to help Sunday School workers understand their witnessing task and to train them how to make teaching, reaching, and ministry contexts for their witnessing.

There are one million Sunday School workers in Southern Baptist churches. Just think what it would mean to the kingdom of our Lord to have such a witnessing army! What outreach possibilities!

Other witness training resources include Equipping Centers and other Church Training materials on witnessing; the age-group "Basic Sunday School Work" books and the "Reaching Series"; and *Every Christian's Job*, written by C. E. Matthews and revised by Bill Hogue and Roy Edgemon—one of the best "how to" books on witnessing.

Continuing training resources are available through the Evangelism Section of the Home Mission Board, the state evangelism directors, and Church Training departments. These resources include the Lay Evangelism Schools, using WIN materials; the TELL witness modules for learner-controlled training; and the new one-on-one approach.

Choice Creations Tracts are available from the Materials Services Department. These would be useful in any witnessing effort.

Department and class activities offer evangelistic opportunities. The Sunday School sponsors many activities in addition to the Sunday morning program—fellowships, socials, banquets, retreats, recreation events, picnics, and class meetings. Often we think of these as being mainly for Sunday School and church members. We often forget to invite prospects to attend or at least we make little effort to lead them to do so. These are activities literally loaded with evangelistic potential. Several hours are involved in a retreat, social, recreation event, or fellowship. On an overnight retreat, for example, what could happen if unsaved friends are present? Can you see the opportunity for genuine care, concern, and verbal witness? It does not mean pressuring the unsaved friend, but offers an opportunity in a natural setting to let members express their love and concern for the person. The unsaved friend has the opportunity in an unpressured situation to see and observe how the members of the Sunday School class act and what kind of persons they are. Structured visitation in the home is essential—and we need more of it—but normally the person visiting has only minutes with the one visited. In a Sunday

School activity, there is more time for building relationships. If the more than 35,000 Sunday Schools catch this concept, the results could prove astonishing and gratifying.

Follow-Up Acts of Concern with Verbal Witness

It is Christlike to help persons in need and distress. When one is hungry, food is needed. When one has no place to sleep, a bed is needed. When one has lost a loved one, understanding and love are needed. When one has lost a job, employment is needed. Whatever the need, it is like Jesus to love, care, and minister to one in need.

But why do we help people in need? Why do we minister, love, care, and give aid? Because it is Christlike, you say? Of course, but the one receiving our help does not always understand that is *why* help is provided. Then *tell* the one helped about Jesus. Witness to him of Jesus. Nearly every opportunity for social ministry is an opportunity for Christian witness. We minister to people because of love; we witness to people because of love.

When people understand who Jesus is and what he does, when they see Christ in us, they often are more receptive to our witness. They will see that to be Christian is not to say only, "Go in peace, be warmed and filled." They will understand that the Christian is willing to help in tangible ways to respond to their hurt. But they also will know that whatever a Christian does, he does it in the name of the Lord. They will know that the Christian cares so much that he wants the unbeliever to know Jesus Christ as Lord.

The one who rightly ministers also shares his faith. He says to the person receiving the ministry: "I want you to know about the good life in Jesus Christ. Let me tell you about him." This kind of witness is the goal of a witnessing Sunday School.

TEACHING TRUTHS ABOUT SALVATION
Laying Foundations

Each age group shares in the total witness of the church and the Sunday School. No one is left out. Consider Preschool workers.

Theirs is the marvelous opportunity of laying the foundation for salvation with boys and girls five years of age and younger. The foundations they lay are used by God when the child reaches the age of accountability.

Preschool workers also have a unique opportunity to witness to unsaved parents of enrolled preschoolers. Visiting in the home, witnessing, and seeking information about the entire family is of great importance. The Preschool teacher often has the best relationship with a lost parent. Both Preschool and Adult workers have a responsibility here and can unite in a team effort to reach unsaved parents.

Telling Children About Salvation

Some children reach accountability during their time in a Children's department. Some do not. We must never believe that we know precisely when a child is accountable to God. We do not; only God knows. Therefore, we should be sensitive about this matter. We should not back away from talking to a child or responding to his questions about salvation, but we shouldn't aggressively move into such conversations. Even in the case of a child who has not reached accountability, Children's workers have the opportunity to lay additional foundation for conversion. As the child continues his Bible study at Sunday School, he is taught how one becomes a Christian. As the child approaches and reaches the point at which under the Spirit's guidance he confronts the demands of Christ on his life, the Children's worker has the unique privilege of working with parents and child. It is desirable that Christian parents have the opportunity of leading their children to Christ. We must remember, however, that not all children have Christian parents; and, if some children come to Christ, it will be because of an influence other than parents.

Children's workers also have a responsibility and privilege of witnessing to unsaved parents of enrolled children. As teachers they should work closely with Adult classes. It is a privilege beyond measure to lead a child's parents to Christ.

Witnessing to Youth

A youth can be won to Christ! Sunday School workers must be highly sensitive to each individual in the class. A worker must never exploit youth. Teachers who really love and are concerned for their pupils will have an appropriate opportunity to witness as they use the curriculum materials. Bible study materials are designed to offer the teacher opportunity to explain the way of salvation. Youth often are led to Christ by a peer. In any case, this period of life is crucial and vital, for several of life's key decisions may be made in this stage. The decision about Christ is the greatest of all decisions.

There is an added evangelistic responsibility for youth workers. Youth not only are led to Christ during this period, but it also is the optimum time for leading them to become witnesses.

Sharing the Gospel of Redemption with Adults

The largest number of unsaved persons in the world are adults. In the past, adults have been slow to respond to Christ. Most Christians accepted Christ as children or youth. There is some evidence that this trend is changing. Adults *are* coming to Christ. Adults are responding to the call to salvation; yet, at this time, there are few unsaved adults in most Sunday School classes. This situation must change. Adult Sunday School classes must discover, enlist, and enroll unsaved adults in Bible classes. Adult members must invite their friends and relatives and do everything possible to enroll them in Bible study. Adult classes must continue in their role of Bible teaching, but they must go beyond it. They must become witnesses to reach men and women of all ages. Adult classes can and should reach lost adults. If the suggestions for organizing for outreach and witnessing and the ideas for implementation are used (chapters 8 and 10), Adult Sunday School members will begin to reach out and witness.

Using Ongoing Curriculum in Evangelism

Ongoing curriculum may be consistently and effectively used

in witnessing and evangelism. Bible texts often contain a full explanation of the way of salvation; while others—in fact, most—convey basic truths related to salvation. If a teacher knows each member of his group and helps members relate Scripture to their needs, possibilities for witnessing are abundant.

A Youth or Adult teacher can lead the study of a biblical text in such a way that the member can understand who Christ is and how to know him. We should aggressively lead unsaved youth and adults to attend our Sunday School classes and teach with the goal of leading those persons to Christ in a salvation experience.

In a Youth or Adult class, a teacher, of course, can offer an invitation to receive Christ. If a lesson offers the opportunity to present the claims of Christ, a teacher may quietly ask the members to bow their heads. The teacher may then ask whether there is one present who wishes to receive Christ or to inquire further about him. After a closing prayer, those who lifted their hands may remain. Other members may quietly move into the worship hour. The teacher can quietly discuss spiritual needs with those who remain. It is one of the basic purposes of the Sunday School to lead persons to respond in faith to Christ. May God grant that it will happen in our Sunday Schools in every one of our more than 35,000 churches.

Workers with children should be alert to answer children's questions that concern their feelings about Christ. The questions may be answered as they arise out of Bible learning activities.

LEADING PERSONS TO RESPOND TO CHRIST IN FAITH
Expressing a Witness That Leads to Responses

It is the privilege and responsibility of Sunday School workers to witness about Jesus Christ. When we visit, it is not enough to visit for our Sunday School class or just for the church. We must visit for Christ. We do not, however, have balance here. Most of our visits are to Baptists with their letters in another church. It is only natural that we talk about the church. Then when we visit a non-Christian, we tend to discuss church membership. We cannot make disciples until we lead someone to Christ. It is not enough that we merely talk about Jesus. We need to tell who he is and what he did. He is the Son of God, the risen Savior. He is Lord. We need to witness with a response in mind. We should witness to win to faith in the Lord Jesus Christ.

Confronting Persons with Their Need to Respond

Our witness to our prospect is incomplete until we talk about his need to respond to Christ. Certainly, pressure is not asked for nor intended, but a clear signal should be given at this point.

GUIDING PERSONS INTO MEANINGFUL CHURCH MEMBERSHIP

When one genuinely receives Jesus Christ as Savior and Lord, joy and obedience are natural responses. Often the new Christian wants to share his new life with others—perhaps his loved ones and friends first. This is natural and right.

In the beginning, the new Christian should learn that he is a part of the body of Christ and, as such, he has privileges and responsibilities. He should be encouraged to unite with a church following conversion. If true conversion is present, so is the desire to obey. Evangelism is not complete, growth has not fully begun, until the new believer becomes a part of the visible body—the church. As the believer follows the Lord in baptism and unites with a local church, he should move into the orientation program for new members. Here he learns about his new life, his church, and his new and exciting responsibilities and privileges. The discipling task includes encouraging new believers to be a part of Church Training and the mission organizations. These will deepen understandings of what it means to be a disciple, to be a part of the people of God. In the regular Bible study and in these organizations, the discipled learn to be disciples. Christian growth begins, and the process in 2 Timothy 2:2 continues.

---

[1]Max L. Caldwell, comp., *Witness to Win* (Nashville: Convention Press, 1978), p. 36.
[2]W. T. Conner, *Christian Doctrine* (Nashville: Broadman Press, 1937), p. 259.

Chapter 10

The Sunday School Is . . . Living the Gospel

"Surely you can see that faith was at work in his actions, and that by these actions the integrity of his faith was fully proved" *(James 2:22, NEB).*

The gospel accepted must be the gospel applied. It must be lived. It must be seen in the flesh. God has sought throughout history to reveal himself to persons. Individuals understood and perceived God best when he came in the flesh in the person of Jesus Christ, and the world will understand and perceive God best when they see Jesus in the lives of Christians.

The Sunday School task of leading persons to live the gospel through loving service and dedicated ministry, through private and public worship, and through regular fellowship with the believers—all in the power of the Holy Spirit—is the subject of this chapter.

LIVING THE GOSPEL THROUGH MINISTERING
Caring, the Christian's Nature

To minister means to meet the needs of persons in the spirit of Christ. It is helping, loving, and caring. Ministering is a natural response because Christians are Christ's people. He is our example. He loved; he cared; he gave; he ministered—so should we. In fact, when we minister to others, we are ministering to him.

This caring task clearly means that Sunday School leaders and members will be involved in helping one another and people in the community. It implies a Christian life-style that is developed and practiced daily by members of class and department groups.

Ministering, a Biblical Imperative

The Sunday School is rightfully and deeply involved in ministering, for Bible study sensitizes believers to the need to minister. Sunday School's small-group approach enables members and prospects to know of one another's needs, and Bible study provides the focal point. The Scripture provides abundant evidence for ministering.

Observe the example of Jesus.—Note the biblical record of how our Lord recognized and ministered to the needs of persons.

- Jesus cleansed a leprous man—Mark 1:41.
- He healed and forgave a paralytic man—Mark 2:1-4.
- He healed a man with a withered hand—Mark 3:5.
- He fed the five thousand—Mark 6:44.
- He made a blind man to see—Mark 8:22-26.
- He cured an epileptic boy—Mark 9:14-29.
- He blessed the little children—Mark 10:13-16.

Note the words of Jesus.—Jesus said that ministering to others is the same as ministering to him: "Then the King will say to those at his right hand, 'Come, O blessed of my Father, inherit the kingdom prepared for you from the foundation of the world; for I was hungry and you gave me food, I was thirsty and you gave me drink, I was a stranger and you welcomed me, I was naked and you clothed me, I was sick and you visited me, I was in prison and you came to me.' Then the righteous will answer him, 'Lord, when did we see thee hungry and feed thee, or thirsty and give thee drink? And when did we see thee a stranger and welcome thee, or naked and clothe thee? And when did we see thee sick or in prison and visit thee?' And the King will answer them, 'Truly, I say to you, as you did it to one of the least of these my brethren, you did it to me' " (Matt. 25:34-40, RSV).

Jesus sent his disciples out, teaching them to "heal the sick, raise the dead, cleanse lepers, cast out demons" (Matt. 10:8, RSV). "Blessed are you poor, for yours is the kingdom of God.

Blessed are you that hunger now, for you shall be satisfied" (Luke 6:20-21, RSV).

See the actions of the early church.—The Macedonian churches took a love offering for the suffering saints in Jerusalem (2 Cor. 8:1-5). Seven men were chosen to minister to some neglected widows (Acts 6:1-3). Peter healed a bedridden man named Aeneas in Lydda (Acts 9:32-35).

Following Christ, a Living Ministry

There is no conflict between serving Christ and helping people. "Surely the Christ who healed the bodies of men and performed a miracle to feed the hungry multitude does not represent a God who is displeased with anything that makes the world a better place in which to live."[1]

Some people believe, however, that a church must decide between winning the lost to Christ and being involved in the application of the gospel. It is not either one or the other; both are essential and are commanded.

Following Christ through loving, serving, and ministering means that Sunday School workers will seek to help persons with emotional needs. Opportunities for ministry are at hand when there is a death in the family, loss of a job, or heartache and difficulties in marriage. Class members and prospects who experience loneliness, confusion, or alienation need a ministry from their class. There also are ministries of celebration in good times. This is Christianity in action.

Being alert to ministering opportunities means being aware of physical hurts and needs also. There may be illness or hospitalization. This is a time when persons need help and are receptive. It is an opportunity for class members to live Christ.

Sunday School classes and departments minister, too. They minister when they share in personal joys of fellow members. Special times for ministry occur when there is a new birth in the family or unique honors have come to members of the class.

When there are conflicts between persons, often the most

effective ministry is a listening ear and an understanding heart. Just to know that someone cares is to receive a ministry.

When Sunday School classes really are Christ's ministers, something happens to those who are ministered to, but something happens also to the one who ministers. The minister experiences personal growth and becomes the receiver.

The real purpose of ministry is to do what Christ would do if he were present in the flesh. It is to support persons in crisis, to offer them help, hope, and encouragement. Ministry may take varied forms, but it always seeks the best for another person. This ministry should be performed wherever a need is discovered.

Sunday School members and workers can help the pastor extend his ministry. They can share information with the pastor concerning persons who need ministry requiring special skills. The pastor can then be responsible for meeting the need personally or engaging the help of persons with special skills or community agencies. Sunday School members and workers also can provide supportive friendship in special types of crises where they are not skilled for ministry. This friendship can reinforce the pastoral ministry extended.

Opportunities for Sunday School Ministry

What are some special ministry opportunities available through Sunday School activities and organizations?

Cradle Roll.—The nature of Cradle Roll is to reach children and families for Christ. In visitation in the home, ample ministry opportunities are readily apparent. When a new child is born, parents are particularly receptive to spiritual ministry.

Bus outreach.—This work provides unique opportunities for ministry, because it involves weekly visits. Often bus routes are in low socioeconomic sections, and it is apparent that persons have a need for clothing, food, and medicine. The need for ministry is clear.

Homebound departments.—Homebound persons often have

need for medicine, food, or transportation. Sometimes they just need to talk. Homebound persons need love and usually are quite receptive to spiritual ministries. Sometimes the best ministry to a homebound person is to find a ministry for him to perform for others.

Vacation Bible School.—This annual project provides entrance into homes beyond regular attenders. Family and individual needs are discovered through follow-up visits in the home. Mission Vacation Bible School and Backyard Bible Clubs offer additional ministry opportunities.

Special groups.—Not every Sunday School can provide Bible study groups for persons with every type of need—blindness, deafness, mental retardation, and so on. But many do, and many also provide Bible study for ethnics who have just arrived in the United States. When Bible study is offered for these groups, many new ministry opportunities become readily apparent. These special persons have unique needs that can be met by sensitive, loving, and caring Sunday School classes, groups, and departments.

LIVING THE GOSPEL THROUGH WORSHIP
Worship, the Christian Response to God's Love

Definition.—In true worship, we respond to almighty God. That response often includes adoration, praise, thanksgiving, confession, exhortation, consecration, and fellowship. Worship means encounter with God. In this encounter, a Christian's faith is deepened and enlightened and his commitment for service is made stronger. Worship not only is encounter with God, it also is fellowship and relationship with man. So worship has both vertical (to God) and horizontal (to man) aspects. Both are important. Worship is foundational in all that a church does. It is the wellspring of a Christian's vitality and commitment.

It most surely is not a casual act. Worship is a deep and natural response of man to God and perhaps one of the highest and holiest of which he is capable. True worship sends us on a redemptive mission. If we truly have had a vision of God we must go forth and share our knowledge of him. The true worshiper can do no less.

Worship in the early church.—Following the example of our Lord (Luke 4:16), the early church met regularly to worship—in the Temple, synagogues, or homes of believers. Later the churches met on the first day of the week (Acts 20:7; 1 Cor. 16:2). Believers were instructed to attend worship (Heb. 10:25).

Encouragement Through the Sunday School

The Sunday School takes a strong and positive stance with regard to worship. One of the Sunday School tasks is to lead its members to worship. The Sunday School hour and the worship hour are inseparably related. They complement each other. One is incomplete without the other. Bible study in Sunday School alone is not enough. Congregational worship by the church family is essential. But it alone is not enough.

The Sunday School not only encourages members to worship in various ways, but it teaches the nature and meaning of worship. It does so through department periods and through a study of worship-related biblical passages.

The Sunday School also provides various opportunities for worship that do not compete with congregational worship but complement it. Such opportunities include department overnight retreats and one-day Bible study worship sessions provided for various Adult groups.

Worship resources available include devotional readings in these periodicals: *encounter!* (for youth), *Open Windows* (regular and large print editions, for adults), and *Home Life* (for families).

Varieties of Worship Needed

Congregational worship.—The Scriptures are absolutely clear. Congregational worship is a fundamental and essential part of the Christian life. All believers are strongly instructed to worship publicly (Heb. 10:25 and 1 Tim. 2:8). The elements of that worship are identified in 1 Timothy 4:13. The book of Revelation pictures the triumphant church engaged in worship in heaven (Rev. 5:9-13; 11:17-18; 15:3-4).

Individual private worship.—The Scriptures are filled with instructions regarding Bible study and prayer. Jesus showed both his familiarity with the Scriptures and his reliance on them. Two notable examples of his feelings about the place of Scripture are in Luke 4:17-21 and Luke 24:32. In the synagogue and on the road to Emmaus, Jesus shared his knowledge of the Scriptures. In Mark 12:24, he said: "Is not this why you are wrong, that you know neither the Scriptures nor the power of God?" (RSV). He quoted the Scriptures often. (See Matt. 4:4,7,10; 7:7; 17:17; John 7:24; 8:35 for examples.)

It is through a study of God's Word, personally applied, that a Christian discovers one of the avenues to Christian growth. Consistent Christians find personal individual Bible study indispensable to their continued growth. Bible study in a Sunday School class is essential, but the maturing, growing Christian needs private individual Bible study, as well.

Prayer is the second and essential part of individual private worship. Just as no one can study the Bible for another person, no one can commune with the Father for another. The Bible is clear about the cruciality of prayer in the Christian life. Prayer is fundamental in both Testaments. "Sometimes it is the cry of a simple soul for some personal boon, as Hannah's (1 Sam. 1:11); sometimes it is the unselfish prayer of Intercession (Gen. 18:23; Ex. 32:31; 1 Sam. 12:23)."[2]

Prayer injunctions and illustrations in the New Testament almost leap out at the reader. Jesus prayed (Matt. 14:23), and he taught his disciples to pray (Matt. 6:9). The early church fervently and consistently prayed (Acts 1:24), and Paul prayed for relief from pain (2 Cor. 12:8).

Prayer and Bible study are necessary in the life of the growing Christian. The best test of this truth is to evaluate it in your own life. Most of us find that when life is dull and lacks spiritual vitality, there is a reason. Often the reason is because of an absence of prayer and Bible study. Every believer ought to have a regular daily time of Bible study and prayer. Growth and maturity always come with faithfulness to this practice. Individual devotional experiences can be enhanced by the use of *Open Windows* and *encounter!*

Family worship.—It is an acknowledged fact that the family in America has experienced severe and tragic erosion. Surely this condition must grieve the heart of our Lord. Surely it is one of the most serious problems in society. The family is the primary unit in biblical material. Jesus spoke of honoring parents (Mark 7:10) and of cleaving to one's wife (Mark 10:7). He said that a divided family cannot stand (Matt. 12:25). Paul talked about the nature and importance of the family (Eph. 5:21 to 6:9).

One of the elements that has contributed throughout history to the stability of Christian families has been the practice of family Bible study and prayer. We have referred to this practice as the "family altar" time. It must be admitted that the pace and manner of life in the 80s is far different from that of other generations. It is difficult to gather the family for a meal. In fact, some families rarely have all members at the table at one time. It is even more difficult to gather them for Bible study and prayer. Yet many Christian families still do so with eternal and wonderful rewards. Whatever the cost, every Christian family should rearrange its schedule to provide for a daily time of family worship. The result is worth it. (*Home Life* magazine contains suggestions for daily family worship.)

LIVING THE GOSPEL THROUGH FELLOWSHIP

Every believer and every Sunday School member needs fellowship. It is a fact of life. It always has been so. There is strength, joy, and sharing in fellowship; it provides meaning and relationship in life. Believers need one another.

Fellowship is an important New Testament word conveying different meanings. Sometimes, it means bearing one another's burdens (Gal. 6:2). Sometimes it means sharing in the suffering of

Christ (Phil. 3:10; Rom. 8:17), or it may be used as the church's fellowship with God (1 John 1:3), with Christ (1 Cor. 1:9), or with the Holy Spirit (2 Cor. 13:14). Elsewhere, it is used for the fellowship of the church (Acts 2:42; Gal. 2:9). It is this latter understanding of the word that we have in mind as we think of the Sunday School class touching lives through fellowship with fellow members.

Individuals need small-group fellowship. The Sunday School class is made to order for creating the small groups within which warm Christian fellowship can take place. The individual class is a remarkable basic unit of fellowship because of the size.

Sunday School classes and departments are ideal for providing activities that foster fellowship. Not only do monthly class meetings provide opportunity for class business and additional Bible study, but there is inherent in class meetings potential for fellowship among members and prospective members. Many classes have found that these meetings have huge outreach potential. Classes and departments also may provide retreats, socials, banquets, and other recreational activities. There is fellowship potential in such activities, but many Sunday School classes and departments also see in them much outreach potential. The activities leader in an Adult class (a newly created position) has a unique responsibility at precisely this point. As Sunday School classes and departments catch the vision of the vast potential for outreach, we will see increasing numbers of Sunday Schools become involved in these productive events.

LIVING THE GOSPEL IN THE POWER OF THE HOLY SPIRIT
Administration—a Spiritual Ministry

Sometimes we forget or neglect the spiritual basis of the ministry involved in administering the multifaceted work of the Sunday School. This is a great error. The effective administration of Sunday School is a deeply spiritual matter. The nature and tasks of the Sunday School underline the spiritual importance of the task. The Bible is taught. The salvation of persons is at stake. Is there anything of greater significance or consequence?

Make no mistake about it, the Sunday School administrative task has a spiritual base, and the gifts to perform the task are provided by the Father. The apostle Paul identified various gifts to the believer in 1 Corinthians 12. He identified "administration" (1 Cor. 12:27) as being one of the God-given gifts. Wherever God's work is to be performed, there is someone with the gift needed to do the work. In every Sunday School, persons should be sought out and enlisted for jobs that fit their gifts. It is important to note that each member of the body has one or more gifts. No man is excluded.

Now if the task is spiritual and the gifts are given, what is the source of power for service? Do the Sunday School workers (the gifted) serve in their own power? Do they depend upon sound organization and wise planning? Can the Sunday School workers effectively serve because of the beautiful and adequate buildings or the adequate provision of space and equipment? Will Sunday School workers be successful because of the carefully coordinated and well-thought-out curriculum? Or will effectiveness be achieved because Sunday School workers have been properly enlisted and adequately trained? The answer is no to all of these—a thousand times no! These elements are absolutely essential; they are basic, but they are not enough. There is one vital and essential ingredient missing. What is it?

The Holy Spirit, the Source of Power for Serving

The essential ingredient in SERVICE is the person of the Holy Spirit, the third person of the Trinity. He is the Paraclete (the one who walks alongside). He is the "Christ in us" found so often in Paul's writings. The Holy Spirit and the "Christ in us" are one and the same. When we refer to "his presence in us" or "his indwelling presence," we mean the same thing. There has been much confusion in terminology about the Holy Spirit, but let us clearly understand that when we refer to any of the above, we refer to the source of power available for one who serves Christ.

The quickest route to failure for a Sunday School teacher, an outreach leader, a Sunday School director, a group leader, or any servant of God is to serve in one's own supposed power or abilities. In truth, we have no power but his power. To be sure, we can "present our bodies a living sacrifice" (Rom. 12:1); we can ask to be his "vessel," and still find ourselves powerless. Over and over Scripture teaches this marvelous truth: The source of power for service is the presence of Christ through the Holy Spirit. Whether the reference is from the Old or New Testament, Holy Spirit power gives strength, courage, and victories. The work is not done in our power, but in the power of God's Spirit.

The Old Testament is filled with that truth. David's words bore clear testimony to his power source: "You come to me with a sword and with a spear and with a javelin; but I come to you in the name of the Lord of hosts" (1 Sam. 17:45, RSV). And again, "that all this assembly may know that the Lord saves not with sword and spear; for the battle is the Lord's and he will give you into our hand" (1 Sam. 17:47, RSV). It is clear again, our power is from God.

The New Testament gives clear testimony to the magnificent truth that the Holy Spirit is our power source. What was the explanation for the "about face" of cowering Peter who had denied Jesus three times only to come back to preach the Pentecostal sermon? It was power—resurrection power—that changed Peter. Peter and John spoke boldly before the Sanhedrin: "Whether it is right in the sight of God to listen to you rather than to God, you must judge; for we cannot but speak of what we have seen and heard" (Acts 4:19, RSV). What enabled them to speak so courageously? The answer is in Acts 4:8, RSV: "Peter, filled with the Holy Spirit." It was the presence of Jesus' resurrection power, the indwelling presence of his Holy Spirit that enabled them to speak and act thusly. It was the same power of which Paul spoke in Ephesians: "This power working in us is the same as the mighty strength which he used when he raised Christ from death" (Eph. 1:19-20, GNB).

Open the pages of the incomparable book. You cannot escape the clear truth that it is Christ's presence and Spirit who provides power. I close this book by citing the words of Jesus himself in the Great Commission: "And lo, I am with you always, to the close of the age" (Matt. 28:20, RSV).

Jesus was saying, in effect: "When you prepare to teach my word, I am with you. When you witness to unsaved friends, I am with you. When you visit someone in the hospital, I am with you. When you minister to the troubled young couple in your class, I am with you. Whatever you do in my name, I am with you."

This magnificent spiritual truth provides no basis for inadequate personal preparation. It provides no basis for a lack of effort, study, or prayer. In the work of reaching, witnessing, teaching, ministering and worshiping, we will do our best to be effective. But in the doing of it, we will recognize that there is only one true power source. It is the presence of the Father in the person of the Holy Spirit. It is "Christ in us." We praise God for this magnificent eternal truth.

My prayer for you who seek to carry out his mission through the Sunday School is that of Paul's for the Ephesians: "That he would grant you according to the riches of His glory, to be strengthened with power through His Spirit in the inner man; so that Christ may dwell in your hearts through faith; . . . . that you may be filled up to all the fulness of God" (Eph. 3:16-19, NASB).

---

[1] W. T. Conner, *Christian Doctrine* (Nashville: Broadman Press, 1937), p. 229.
[2] H. H. Rainley, *Short Dictionary of Bible Themes* (New York: Basic Books, Inc., 1968), p. 72.

RESOURCES FOR SUNDAY SCHOOL WORK

All of these materials not designated otherwise are available from Baptist Book Stores. Items marked "MSD" may be purchased from Materials Services Department, Sunday School Board, Nashville, Tennessee 37234.

BOOKS

Basic Series:
 Basic Sunday School Work
 Basic Adult Sunday School Work
 Basic Youth Sunday School Work
 Basic Children's Sunday School Work
 Basic Preschool Work

Bible Survey Series:
 An Introduction to the Bible
 How to Study the Bible
 A Nation in the Making
 Israel's Period of Progress
 The Centuries of Decline
 The Life and Ministry of Our Lord
 The Growth of the Early Church
 Messages from First-century Christians
Bible Teaching Program Plan Book (annual editions)
Every Christian's Job (written originally by C. E. Matthews; revised by Bill Hogue and Roy Edgemon)
How to Improve Bible Teaching and Learning in Sunday School: Pastor-Director Guide
Reaching and Teaching Mentally Retarded Persons

Reaching Series:
  Reaching People Through the Sunday School
  Reaching Adults Through the Sunday School
  Reaching Youth Through the Sunday School
  Reaching Children Through the Sunday School
  Reaching Preschoolers
Sunday School Director's Handbook

Teaching Series:
  Helping Teachers Teach
  Teaching Adults in Sunday School
  Teaching Youth in Sunday School
  Teaching Children in Sunday School
  Teaching Preschoolers
The Baptist Faith and Message
Training Outreach Workers for the Sunday School
Training Potential Sunday School Workers
Witness to Win
Working with Homebound Adults in Sunday School
Working with Senior Adults in Sunday School
Working with Single Adults in Sunday School

Youth Sunday School Leadership Development Series:
  Pak 1: Developing Teaching Skills
  Pak 2: Developing Learner-Involvement Skills (available April 1981)
  Pak 3: Developing Reaching Skills (available April 1982)

KITS

Adult Class Leader Administration Kit
Adult Class Prospect Visitation Kit

Basic Series:
  Basic Sunday School Work: Resource Kit
  Basic Adult Sunday School Work: Resource Kit

Basic Youth Sunday School Work: Resource Kit
Basic Children's Sunday School Work: Resource Kit
Basic Preschool Work: Resource Kit
Bible Survey Series Teaching Resource Kit

Reaching Series:
Reaching People Through the Sunday School: Resource Kit
Reaching Adults Through the Sunday School: Resource Kit
Reaching Youth Through the Sunday School: Resource Kit
Reaching Children Through the Sunday School: Resource Kit
Reaching Preschoolers: Resource Kit
Sunday School Preparation Week: Resource Kit

Teaching Series:
Helping Teachers Teach: Resource Kit
Teaching Adults in Sunday School: Resource Kit
Teaching Youth in Sunday School: Resource Kit
Teaching Children in Sunday School: Resource Kit
Teaching Preschoolers: Resource Kit
Training Sunday School Workers in Outreach (Equipping Center—MSD)
Workers' Meeting Resource Kit (quarterly—MSD)
Working with Senior Adults in Sunday School: Resource Kit
Working with Single Adults in Sunday School: Resource Kit
Youth Are Witnesses, Too Packet

PERIODICALS

Adult Leadership (MSD)
Children's Leadership (MSD)
encounter! (MSD)
Home Life (MSD)
Motivators for Sunday School Workers (MSD)
Open Windows (MSD)
Preschool Leadership (MSD)
Sunday School Leadership (MSD)

RECORD FORMS
Broadman Revised Sunday School Record System
Preschool:
  Baby's Schedule Card (Form 9)
  Attendance Record (Form 6)
  Sunday School Member's Report Envelope (Form 103-S)*
  Member's Record (Form 105-S)
  Summary of Weekly Records (Form 106-S)
  Sunday School Record Covers (Form 107-S)

Children:
  Attendance Record (Form 6)
  Sunday School Member's Report Envelope (Form 103-S)*
  Member's Record (Form 105-S)
  Summary of Weekly Records (Form 106-S)
  Sunday School Record Covers (Form 107-S)

Youth:
  Sunday School Member's Report Envelope (Form 103-S)*
  Member's Record (Form 105-S)
  Summary of Weekly Records (Form 106-S)
  Sunday School Record Covers (Form 107-S)

Adult:
  Sunday School Member's Report Envelope (Form 103-S)*
  Member's Record (Form 105-S)
  Summary of Weekly Records (Form 106-S)
  Sunday School Record Covers (Form 107-S)
  Department/School Weekly Report Card (Form 110-S)

School:
  Sunday School Member's Report Envelope (Form 103-S)*
  Member's Record (Form 105-S)

Summary of Weekly Records (Form 106-S)
Sunday School Record Covers (Form 107-S)
School Triplicate Report Book (Form 181-S) Revised or (Form 184-S) Revised

Broadman Sunday School Six Point Record System
Preschool:
Baby's Schedule Card (Form 9)
Child's Attendance Record (Form 470)
Individual Report Envelope (Form 15)*
Individual Record Card (Form 405Y)
Summary of Weekly Record (Form 410Q)
Sunday School Record Covers

Children:
Child's Attendance Record (Form 470)
Individual Report Envelope (Form 15)*
Individual Record Card (Form 405Y)
Summary of Weekly Record (Form 410Q)
Sunday School Record Covers

Youth:
Individual Report Envelope (Form 15)*
Individual Record Card (Form 405Y)
Summary of Weekly Record (Form 410Q)
Sunday School Record Covers

Adult:
Individual Report Envelope (Form 15)*
Individual Record Card (Form 405Y)
Summary of Weekly Record (Form 410Q)
Sunday School Record Covers

School:
Individual Report Envelope (Form 15)*

Individual Record Card (Form 405Y)
Summary of Weekly Record (Form 410Q)
School Triplicate Report Book (No. 3)

Other Forms
Cradle Roll:
Cradle Roll Member's Record (Form 26)
Cradle Roll Group Enrollment (Form 25)
Cradle Roll Monthly Report (Form 24)
Sunday School Record Card Covers (Form 107-S) or Sunday
    School Record Covers

Outreach, Enrollment, and Record Correction:
People Search Family Card
Prospect File Card (Form 5)
Visitation Assignment (Form 3)
Enrollment Prospect Visitation Assignment and Report (Form
    120)
Prospect Assignment Pocket and Card (MSD)
Triplicate Registration Record (Form 2)
Enrollment Card (Form 10)
Record Correction (Form 4)
Personal Record Folder for Teachers and Leaders

*Many Southern Baptist churches use Printed-to-Order Church
Offering Envelopes. These envelopes can be boxed and dated
consecutively for each Sunday of the year. They are available in
both the Revised Sunday School Record System and the Sunday
School Six Point Record System, through the Baptist Book Store
Envelope Service. More complete information can be obtained
by writing to Baptist Book Store Envelope Service, Box 193,
Chester, West Virginia 26034.

PERSONAL LEARNING ACTIVITIES

Chapter 1

1. Identify a word or phrase to describe or illustrate each of the five concepts embodied in the nature of the church.

2. How would you define the mission of the church? What is the importance of the Bible in understanding the mission of the church?

3. The writer says, "Our mission is *for* Christ, *in* love, and *to* persons." To see persons as Jesus saw them, what do you think Christian leaders must do to respond in love?

4. Look over the reasons that the Sunday School is well equipped to serve as the major outreach organization of the church. Identify at least one reason where you and your church may need to give more attention.

Chapter 2

1. Indicate one significant contribution or happening for each of the Flake, Barnette, Washburn periods in the historical roots of the Sunday School movement.

2. Look at the tasks of the Sunday School. For each task, suggest a word or phrase that interprets the work of the Sunday School.

3. In fifty words or less, paraphrase Harry Piland's vision. What is your vision of what can happen in your church through its Sunday School?

Chapter 3

1. List some reasons for having organization in the Sunday School.

2. What are the three major structures through which Sunday

School work is done?

3. What are three suggested guidelines for each of the four age divisions in organizing Sunday School work?

4. What are some ways to use records?

5. Why is the pastor the key to effective organization?

6. How do you respond personally to values of annual promotion as listed in this chapter? Identify one positive and one negative response.

7. Look at the guidelines for considering organization options. With your type situation (small, middle sized, large, inner-city, mission) in mind, list those that seem similar to your situation.

8. What is the timeless formula for Sunday School organization?

Chapter 4

1. How do you feel about the qualities and characteristics of a Sunday School leader? In your opinion, which of the characteristics is most often overlooked in worker enlistment? Why?

2. In the section or sections related to your job assignments, name at least two of your responsibilities.

3. What are the major sources for compiling and listing potential workers? What are your suggestions for using the series of questions about each church member?

4. List some ideas to develop motivation within persons. From your list, explain how one approach was used effectively with *you* by another leader.

5. Check the requirements for credit on a Sunday School Leadership diploma. Since this is one of the required books, when do you expect to receive your diploma?

Chapter 5

1. Several groups are identified as planning groups. Describe one thing that actually happens in each one.

2. What are some ways Standards can be used by the Sunday School, by departments, and by classes?

3. Prepare a list of ways plans are communicated. Circle those that are used in your church.

Chapter 6

1. Dr. Piland suggests that solid weekly workers' meetings will produce better teachers and greater successes in reaching people. Do you agree? disagree? Why?

2. Outline the steps general officers should take to begin weekly workers' meetings.

3. If you are from a small Sunday School, what are some suggestions for conducting the meeting in small Sunday Schools?

4. Identify two things that actually happen:
   a. In the department directors' period.
   b. In the general period.
   c. In the department period—administering department concerns.
   d. In the department period—planning for teaching-learning.

Chapter 7

1. Identify some biblical references to reaching. Which passage has a particular tug at your heart? Why?

2. List groups of special people your church should attempt to reach. Check those for which some provision is made in your church. Circle those where no provision presently exists for persons with special needs. Investigate further *one* of those circled about what possibly could be done by the beginning of the new church year.

3. What responsibility do Sunday School workers and members have in visiting, contacting, and enrolling prospects?

Chapter 8

1. Prepare a chart with headings as shown. Look through the chapter and insert appropriate words and phrases in the two columns.

NEEDS	HOW LEARNED

Preschoolers
Children
Youth
Adult

2. What, if anything, impressed you about the basic guidelines followed by persons who design Sunday School Bible study materials?

3. What one new thought surfaced from your reading the age-group suggestions under "Teaching Requires the Proper Setting"?

Chapter 9

1. Select one New Testament example of a verbal witness. Write a brief, first-person monologue or statement of what the early witness probably said and felt.

2. List some ways in which churches can sensitize members to be aware of unsaved persons?

3. How do departments and classes offer evangelistic opportunities?

4. In order to lead someone to Christ, what must leaders and members do beyond merely talking about Jesus or the church?

Chapter 10

1. Why is the caring or ministering task such an integral part of the Sunday School.

2. How do Sunday School classes and departments foster fellowship?

3. Recognizing that the Holy Spirit is our power source, write out a personal prayer from you—a Sunday School leader—regarding your own Sunday School responsibility.

The Church Study Course

The Church Study Course consists of a variety of short-term credit courses for adults and youth and noncredit foundational units for children and preschoolers. The materials are for use in addition to the study and training curriculums made available to the churches on an ongoing basis.

Study courses and foundational units are organized into a system that is promoted by the Sunday School Board, 127 Ninth Avenue, North, Nashville, Tennessee 37234; by the Woman's Missionary Union, 600 North Twentieth Street, Birmingham, Alabama 35203; by the Brotherhood Commission, 1548 Poplar Avenue, Memphis, Tennessee 38104; and by the respective departments of the state conventions affiliated with the Southern Baptist Convention.

Study course materials are flexibile enough to be adapted to the needs of any Baptist church. The resources are published in several different formats—textbooks of various sizes, workbooks, and kits. Each item contains a brief explanation of the Church Study Course and information on requesting credit. Additional information and interpretation are available from the participating agencies.

Types of Study and Credit

Adults and youth can earn study course credit through individual or group study. Teachers of courses or of foundational units also are eligible to receive credit.

1. Class Experience.—Group involvement with course material for the designated number of hours for the particular course. A person who is absent from one or more sessions must complete the "Personal Learning Activities" or other requirements for the material missed.
2. Individual Study.—This includes reading, viewing, or listening to course material and completing the specified

requirements for the course.

3. Lesson Course Study.—Parallel use of designated study course material during the study of selected units in Church Program Organization periodical curriculum units. Guidance for this means of credit appears in the selected periodical.

4. Institutional Study.—Parallel use of designated study course material during regular courses at educational institutions, including Seminary Extension Department courses. Guidance for this means of credit is provided by the teacher.

Credit is awarded for the successful completion of a course of study. This credit is granted by the Church Study Course Awards Office, 127 Ninth Avenue, North, Nashville, Tennessee 37234, for the participating agencies. Form 151 (available free) is recommended for use in requesting credit.

When credit is issued to a person on request, the Awards Office sends two copies of a notice of credit earned to the church. The original copy of the credit slip should be filed by the study course clerk in the participant's record of training folder. The duplicate should be given to the person who earned the credit. Accumulated credits are applied toward leadership or member development diplomas, which are measures of learning, growth, development, and training.

Detailed information about the Church Study Course system of credits, diplomas, and record keeping is available from the participating agencies. Study course materials, supplementary teaching or learning aids, and forms for record keeping may be ordered from Baptist Book Stores.

The Church Study Course Curriculum

Credit is granted on those courses listed in the current copy of *Church Services and Materials Catalog, Church Study Course Catalog,* and *Baptist Book Store Catalog.* When selecting courses or foundational units, check the current catalogs to determine what study course materials are valid.

How to Request Credit for This Course

This book is the text for a course in the subject area Sunday School Leadership.

This course is designed for 5 hours of group study. Credit is awarded for satisfactory class experience with the study material for the minimum number of hours. A person who is absent from one or more sessions must complete the "Personal Learning Activities" or other requirements for the materials missed.

Credit is also allowed for use of this material in individual study and in institutional study, if so designated by an educational institution.

After the course is completed, the teacher, the study course clerk, or any person designated by the church should complete Form 151 ("Church Study Course Credit Request, Revised 1975") and send it to the Awards Office, 127 Ninth Avenue, North, Nashville, Tennessee 37234. Individuals also may request credit by writing the Awards Office. The form on the next page may be used.

CHURCH STUDY COURSE CREDIT REQUEST, REVISED 1975

THE SUNDAY SCHOOL BOARD OF THE SOUTHERN BAPTIST CONVENTION

NOTE: Material for each course gives the requirements to be met before credit is requested. See the *Church Study Course Catalog* for additional information.

Prepare duplicate copy for Church's Record
Please print or type. Do not write in shaded areas.

State Convention		Association			Indicate Type of Study (X)
					☐ Class ☐ Individual ☐ Lesson Course ☐ Educational Institution

CHURCH

Church Name	Mail to (If Different from Church Address)
Mailing Address	Street, Route, or P. O. Box
City, State, Zip Code	City, State, Zip Code

MAIL TO

LAST NAME	FIRST NAME AND MIDDLE INITIAL	MRS. (X)	COURSE TITLE
1			Basic Sunday School Work
2			
3			
4			
5			
6			
7			
8			

MAIL THIS REQUEST TO	CHURCH STUDY COURSE AWARDS OFFICE RESEARCH SERVICES DEPARTMENT 127 NINTH AVENUE, NORTH NASHVILLE, TENNESSEE 37234	Signature of Pastor, Teacher, or Study Leader	Date

FORM 151 (Rev. 8-75)